The Observing Self

The
Observing Self

Mysticism
and Psychotherapy

Arthur J. Deikman, M.D.

Beacon Press   Boston

Grateful acknowledgment is given to the following for permission to reprint: Martin Buber's "His Own Suffering." Reprinted by permission of Schocken Books Inc. from *Tales of the Hasidim: Early Masters* by Martin Buber. Copyright © 1947 by Schocken Books Inc. Copyright renewed © 1975 by Schocken Books Inc.; Martin Buber's "The Treasure." Reprinted by permission of Schocken Books Inc. from *Tales of the Hasidim: Later Masters* by Martin Buber. Copyright © 1948 by Schocken Books Inc. Copyright renewed © 1975 by Schocken Books Inc.; Rainer Maria Rilke's "The Archaic Torso of Apollo." "Archaic Torso of Apollo" is reprinted from *Translations from the Poetry of Rainer Maria Rilke* by M. D. Herter Norton by permission of W. W. Norton & Company, Inc. Copyright 1938 by W. W. Norton & Company, Inc. Copyright renewed 1966 by M. D. Herter Norton; Idries Shah's *Thinkers of the East*, © Idries Shah 1971, by permission of the author; Idries Shah's *The Magic Monastery*, © Idries Shah 1972, by permission of the author; Idries Shah's *The Exploits of the Incomparable Mulla Nasrudin*, © Mulla Nasrudin Enterprises Ltd 1966, by permission of the author; Idries Shah's *The Pleasantries of the Incredible Mulla Nasrudin*, © Mulla Nasrudin Enterprises Ltd 1968, by permission of the author; Idries Shah's *The Wisdom of Idiots*, © Idries Shah 1969, by permission of the author; Idries Shah's *The Way of the Sufi*. From *The Way of the Sufi* by Idries Shah. Copyright © 1968 by Idries Shah. Reprinted by permission of the publisher, E. P. Dutton, Inc.; Idries Shah's *Tales of the Dervishes*. From *Tales of the Dervishes* by Idries Shah. Copyright © 1967 by Idries Shah. Reprinted by permission of the publisher, E. P. Dutton, Inc.

Beacon Press books are published under the auspices
of the Unitarian Universalist Association,
25 Beacon Street, Boston, Massachusetts 02108
Published simultaneously in Canada by
Fitzhenry & Whiteside Limited, Toronto

Printed in the United States of America

(paperback) 9 8

Library of Congress Cataloging in Publication Data

Deikman, Arthur.
    The observing self.

      1. Mysticism — Psychological aspects.
2. Psychotherapy.   I. Title.
BL625.D39   291.4'2   81-70486
ISBN 0-8070-2951-3   AACR2

Preface

For a number of years I have been investigating the mystical tradition, attempting to understand it from the perspective of modern psychology, especially developmental psychology and psychodynamic theory. As a result I now regard mysticism as a type of science devoted to a practical goal, one important to Western culture and the practice of psychotherapy. I have also come to see that mysticism, particularly in the West, is greatly misunderstood, which has interfered with our learning how mysticism can increase the effectiveness of psychotherapy and deepen our understanding of human life.

It is hard to write about the mystical tradition's relation to psychotherapy because the two subjects are vast and multifaceted. In addition, aspects of each are difficult to comprehend without direct experience and few people have extensive knowledge of both realms. To complicate matters, partisans of each domain tend to regard those of the other as self-deluded. Many physical scientists and psychologists view mysticism as a carryover from the Dark Ages and a threat to scientific progress. Those interested in "higher consciousness" often adopt a patronizing, contemptuous attitude toward psychiatry and psychotherapy. A person who writes approvingly of both disciplines is apt to encounter the fate of William Carlos Williams, who complained that in being both a physician and a poet, his membership in one group resulted in his dismissal by the other.

Still, it is possible to understand mystical science in Western psychological terms and *The Observing Self* attempts to provide a framework for doing so. Esoteric religious terminology is not necessary to express what mysticism is about. In the past, such language was used as a matter of social necessity or convenience. Linking mysticism to religion is not essential and is in fact a hindrance in a modern culture whose approach to nature and human experience is through the physical sciences and psychology.

It is my hope that by providing this contemporary framework Western psychological science will be able to make use of the perspective and knowledge of mysticism. This will aid in our developing a more comprehensive and effective understanding of human beings, their suffering, happiness, and fulfillment. My aim is not to instruct our readers in how to adapt mystical techniques to psychotherapy. Such applications would be inappropriate for most therapists and patients. At this stage, the value of the mystical tradition for the Westerner is in the perspective provided on the self and human purpose. This understanding can inform and orient therapists so that, without departing from standard psychotherapeutic procedures, they can effect improved outcomes. I have written *The Observing Self* not only for the mental health professional, but also for the general reader interested in a clearer understanding of both psychotherapy and mysticism.

Assuming that most readers will know considerably more about psychotherapy than about mysticism, I have placed greater emphasis on the latter. Since both psychotherapy and mysticism are as wide and complex as human life itself, a complete description of either is outside the scope of this book. I have therefore focused on ideas that can serve as a bridge between these two spheres of knowledge.

Acknowledgments

The writing of this book was aided by a grant from the Commonwealth Fund and by the administrative assistance of the Langley Porter Institute. Eugene Brody, M.D., provided special help and encouragement in undertaking the project, as did Robert Wallerstein, M.D.

Helpful comments and suggestions were made by a number of persons who read the manuscript or portions of it at various stages of its development: Arthur Colman, M.D.; Etta Deikman; Gordon Globus, M.D.; Silas Hoadley; Lynn Howard; Joanne Kamiya; John Levy; John Mack, M.D.; Michael Murphy; Robert Ornstein, Ph.D.; Donald Sandner, M.D.; Stephen Schoen, M.D.; Ronald Spinka, M.D.; and Robert Wallerstein, M.D. John Levy and Michael Murphy were especially generous in their assistance.

Suzanne Lipsett and Marie Cantlon provided crucial editorial suggestions for which I am very grateful.

I am also grateful to Fred Hill for his steadfast commitment to this work and his skill in guiding it to publication.

To my mother,
Elsie Deikman,
1903–1979

VOICE IN THE NIGHT

A voice whispered to me last night:
"There is no such thing as a voice whispering in the night!"

— Haidar Ansari

Contents

1

An Invitation

PSYCHOTHERAPY

Psychotherapy arose in response to human suffering, and, as far as we can tell, human suffering has always existed. The ancient lineage of psychotherapy is seldom appreciated because Western culture considers psychotherapy as a relatively recent development of psychiatry, one of its subdivisions. If we define psychotherapy as the treatment of mental distress through psychological means, we find records of such practices from the origins of civilization whenever priests, shamans, and witch doctors appear. While psychiatry, a category of scientific medicine, is a modern development, psychotherapy has been associated with the sacred for thousands of years. Historians of psychotherapy acknowledge priests and shamans as the first to heal the psyche. A sorcerer, his head crowned with deer's antlers, is depicted on the wall of a cave in southern France, dating from 15,000 B.C.[1] Psychotherapists of one sort or another have been around a long time.

Formal psychotherapy originated in the eighteenth and nineteenth centuries, when treatment was taken over from the clergy by rationalistic medicine and eventually became

1

the specialty of psychiatry. Psychiatry at first dealt primarily with madness, but Freud's psychoanalysis extended psychiatry and psychotherapy to neurotic and character problems as well. The scope of formal psychotherapy has been progressively enlarged and is now concerned with problems of existential human suffering, the traditional domain of religion, from which psychotherapy historically originated.

Psychotherapy appears to have come full circle. Although the modern version is quite different from the archaic ceremonies that featured magic, taboos, gods, and dramatic rituals of exorcism, there have been changes other than appearance. Its marriage to rational medicine has given psychotherapy a systematic understanding of neurotic and psychotic syndromes and refined technical procedures. And an entirely new dimension, the enhancement of the observing self, has been added.

However, Western science is characterized by a split between the sacred and the rational, which has left modern psychotherapy less well equipped than the superseded ancient, primitive versions to handle certain problems. The loss of dramatic placebo devices is not the difficulty. The issue goes deeper, involving the most fundamental assumptions of Western thought. Freud's view of reality and that of most contemporary theorists of psychotherapy is based on a nineteenth-century physical and biological scientific model that is far too narrow to encompass human consciousness. Consequently, certain sources of suffering cannot be dealt with from within a Western framework. We are faced with major problems that call for broadening our perspective and extending our science.

THE MYSTICAL TRADITION

The mystical tradition is also ancient in origin. The oral teachings recorded in the Upanishads, Buddhist sutras, and similar records go back thousands of years and provide evidence that mystical teachers of widely different cultures say remarkably similar things. Also concerned with human suffering, they propose that human beings are ignorant of their true nature and that ignorance leads to lives of pain and futility. The sages describe a Way that leads to a higher level of existence, one infinitely more desirable than the level on which most people conduct their lives. The mystical tradition does not offer therapy in the usual sense of that word, but achieving the goal of mysticism — experiencing the Real Self — is said to cure human suffering because its very basis is thereby removed.

Often confused with religion, the mystical tradition occupies a place of its own. Durkheim suggested that human beings developed religions through their perception of the sacred, a superior realm impalpable through the five senses but one that can nevertheless be experienced.[2] Religion and mysticism are both concerned with the sacred realm, but most religions tend to associate the sacred with a deity, whereas mysticism associates the sacred with the unrecognized Real Self of each human being. Thus, followers of formal religions often try to affect the behavior of a god — propitiating, pleasing, and seeking aid. In contrast, the mystical tradition asserts the equation: I (Real Self) = God. While "I am God" is the fundamental realization of mysticism, it is blasphemous in many religions.

Because both religion and mysticism respond to the perception of the sacred, the work of mystics historically took place within a religious context although it remained distinct from the activities of everyday religious practices. For example, the wandering monks for whom the Upanishads were written did not perform Hindu sacrifices and rituals, but followed special practices imparted in secret by their teacher.

The monks, usually thought of by laypersons as part of an established religious tradition, were actually following a teaching that said the ordinary forms and concepts of that religion were illusions one must transcend. A similar situation prevailed for Zen monks who pursued their training in the context of Buddhism.

Western culture often overlooks the distinction between religion and mysticism, especially in the psychological and psychiatric literature. This is unfortunate because the mystical emphasis on self-development makes it consonant with modern psychotherapy. The mystical tradition has been concerned with the very problems that modern psychotherapy has been unable to resolve. It makes sense, therefore, to investigate mysticism with a view to dealing more effectively with those problems and gaining wisdom as human beings.

THE PROBLEM OF MEANING

Human beings need meaning. Without it they suffer boredom, depression, and despair. Increasingly, psychotherapists are called on to deal with these symptoms as people confront aging and death in the context of a society that is coming to realize the possibility of its own decline and extinction. The religious framework that formerly defined meaning has been replaced by a scientific world view in which meaning does not exist. "What is the purpose of human life?" and "Why am I?" are questions that are said by most scientists to lie outside the scope of science or to be false, since they assume that the human species developed by chance in a random universe. According to this view, human beings are complex biochemical phenomena, of considerable scientific interest but not essentially different from anything else that science examines.

Western psychotherapy is hard put to meet human beings' need for meaning, for it attempts to understand clinical phenomena in a framework, based on scientific materialism, in which meaning is arbitrary and purpose nonexistent. Consequently, Western psychotherapy interprets the search for meaning as a function of childlike dependency wishes and fears of helplessness or, at best, a genetic disposition toward intellectual control, preserved and enhanced by natural selection because of its survival value.

Such explanations, however tidy they may be, do not offer much help to adolescents and young adults seeking a life path, to persons confronting the anxieties of the nuclear age, or to those who experience despair as death approaches, unable to find significance in life goals based on personal acquisition, unable to find meaning in the purposeless universe of scientific empiricism. Not only are patients affected; psychotherapists fall prey to the same ailment. Consider the following extract from an article in the *American Journal of Psychiatry* reporting the experience of a group of therapists, aged thirty-five to forty-five, most of whom had a psychoanalytic background. The group met ostensibly to obtain peer supervision but soon became a therapy group to deal with a crisis all the members were experiencing:

The original members of the group were remarkably homogeneous in their purpose in joining. The conscious reason was to obtain help in mastering a phase in their own development, the mid-life crisis. We refer to that stage of life in which the individual is aware that half of his time has been used up and the general pattern of trajectory of his work and personal life is clear. At this time, one must give up the normal defenses of early life—infinite faith in one's abilities and the belief that anything is possible. The future becomes finite, childhood fantasies have been fulfilled or unrealized, and there is no longer a sense of having enough time for anything. One becomes aware that one's energy and physical and mental abilities will be declining. The individual must think of prolonging and conserving rather than expanding. The reality of one's limited life span comes into sharp focus, and the work of mourning the passing of life begins in earnest.[3]

This depressed, resigned outlook should not be dismissed as peculiar to that particular group; it is, in fact, an approved psychiatric standard. *The American Handbook of Psychiatry* articulates its contemporary "wisdom" as follows:

> To those who have obtained some wisdom in the process of reaching old age, death often assumes meaning as the proper outcome of life. It is nature's way of assuring more life and constant renewal. Time and customs change but the elderly tire of changing; it is time for others to take over, and the elderly person is willing to pass quietly from the scene.[4]

Here, the meaning of life is death, which provides an end to the fatigue of the elderly. What a vision!

The greatest problem Western psychotherapists face may be the absence of a theoretical framework to provide meaning for patients and therapists alike. Clearly, those struggling to overcome neurotic problems are likely to be badly handicapped when the context within which they view themselves provides neither meaning, direction, nor hope. It is also clear that science's vision of an orderly, mechanical, indifferent universe can provide no purpose for life. Yet our lives and our psychological health depend on a sense of purpose. Mere survival is a purpose, but not enough for human consciousness. Nor is working for the survival of others sufficiently meaningful if one believes that the human race has no place to go, that it endlessly repeats the same patterns, or worse.

The "midlife" crisis with which the psychotherapists grappled probably reflects the fact that at midlife one's own

death becomes less theoretical and more probable. Goals of
money, security, fame, sex, or power might formerly have
given purpose to life. With experience, the limited nature of
such satisfactions becomes increasingly evident. As one grows
older an awareness surfaces that one is on a relentless slide
toward extinction, making self-serving goals seem utterly
futile. Even altruistic goals can wear thin without a larger
picture of the human race than the one our scientific
culture provides. As life progresses, the search for meaning becomes increasingly urgent. Profound despair and
dull resignation are symptoms of failing in that search.
The pervasive use of alcohol, sedatives, and narcotics
in our society might well reflect many people's attempts to
suppress despair at their purposelessness, to substitute
heightened sensation for meaning.

This widespread malady need not be inevitable, for it is
possible that the conclusions of scientific materialism are
wrong. From time to time we sense a larger reality than the
one science provides, a subtle perception pointing to a better,
meaningful existence. The dissonance between the scientific
view and the one we intuit produces restlessness and a need
for resolution. Even the pursuit of material goals may be a
blind response to the urge to attain a dimly sensed reality in
which purpose and meaning are facts, not fantasies. Our ability
to progress in that direction is severely hampered by our
not understanding the nature of the problem, by restricting
reality to the empirical realm. Indeed, Western psychological
science tends to regard the very consciousness through which
we know the physical world to be no more than a product of
that world, an epiphenomenon less real than that which it
comprehends. No wonder meaning vanishes. A physicist
commented on this assumption:

Most painful is the absolute silence of all our scientific investigations towards our questions concerning the meaning and scope of the whole display. The more attentively we watch it, the more aimless and foolish it appears to be. The show that is going on obviously acquires a meaning only with regard to the mind that contemplates it. But what science tells us about this relationship is patently absurd; as if the mind had only been produced by that very display that it is now watching and would pass away with it when the sun finally cools down and the earth has turned into a desert of ice and snow.[5]

It is as if Descartes had been stood on his head and made to declare, "I think; therefore, the world exists and I am an illusion."

Pain and dysfunction inevitably result from the denial or distortion of reality, a consequence clearly demonstrated in the effects of the fantasies of those suffering from psychosis or neurosis. It is equally true of the fantasies and beliefs promulgated by an entire culture. Our culture's belief in positivistic empiricism — only the tangible is real — produces increasing symptoms at the individual, social, and political levels. A person who seeks psychotherapy may be suffering from a distortion of reality not only at the interpersonal but at the metaphysical level, and neither the person nor the psychotherapist is aware of that.

A basic tenet of mysticism is that reality as ordinarily perceived is indeed a distortion and that human suffering is the consequence of believing in that distorted view. According to mystics, the problem is compounded by human beings' inherent need to progress in their ability to perceive the reality that underlies the phenomenal world, which can result only from the development of a higher intuitive faculty, a process called "conscious evolution." People whose evolutionary need is frustrated experience a persistent dissatisfaction with the course of their lives. On the other hand, fulfillment of that developmental goal enables people to perceive the meaning of their own lives and the purpose of human existence. Thus, in the mystical tradition, meaning is a *perceptual* issue.

The problem of limited perception — as encountered in biology — has been described by C. F. Pantin:

> . . . if you are not careful, you may start to imagine that you can explain the whole behavior of the sea anemone by very simple reflexes — like the effect of a coin in a slot machine. But quite by accident, I discovered that apart from reflexes, there was a whole mass of purposive behavior connected with the spontaneous activity of the anemone about which we simply know nothing. (Actually, this behavior was too slow to be noticed; it was outside our sensory spectrum for the time being.)[6]

Similarly, it is possible that the meaning and purpose of human life are outside the spectrum of ordinary consciousness, whose widening and deepening are the concern of the mystical tradition. In fact, some see the evolution of consciousness as the principal task of the human race. Western psychology, in its often vain attempts to explain away the sense of meaninglessness and its attendant symptoms, may have much to learn from mysticism, which sees meaning as something real and accessible to consciousness, provided the appropriate perceptual capacity has been developed.

THE OBSERVING SELF

The fundamental questions, "Who am I?" and "What am I?" arise increasingly in the struggle to find meaning and purpose in life. Therapists hear them as explicit queries or in indirect form: "Who is the *real* me?" or "I don't know what I want — part of me wants one thing and part of me wants something else. What do *I* want?" Western psychology is severely handicapped in dealing with these questions because the center of human experience — the observing self — is missing from its theories. Yet, at the heart of psychopathology lies a fundamental confusion between the self as object and the self of pure subjectivity. Emotions, thoughts, impulses, images, and sensations are the *contents* of consciousness: we witness them; we are aware of their existence. Likewise, the body, the self-image, and the self-concept are all constructs that we *observe*. But our core sense of personal existence — the "I" — is located in awareness itself, not in its content.

The distinction between awareness and the content of awareness tends to be ignored in Western psychology, its implications for our everyday life are not appreciated. Indeed, most people have trouble recognizing the difference between awareness and content, which are part of everyday life. Yet, careful observation shows people that they can suspend their thoughts, that they can experience silence or darkness and the temporary absence of images or memory patterns — that any element of mental life can disappear while awareness itself remains. Awareness is the ground of conscious life, the background or field in which all elements exist, different from thoughts, sensations, or images. One can experience the distinction simply by looking straight ahead. Be aware of what you experience, then close your eyes. Awareness remains. "Behind" your thoughts and images is awareness, and that is where *you* are.

What we know as our self is separate from our thoughts, memories, feelings, and any content of consciousness. No Western psychological theory concerns itself with this fundamental fact; all describe the self in terms of everything but the observer, who is the center of

all experience. This crucial omission stems from the fact
that the observing self is an anomaly — not an object, like
everything else. Our theories are based on objects: we
think in terms of objects, talk in terms of objects. It is
not just the physical world that we apprehend in that way;
the elements of our mental life are similar. Seemingly diffuse and amorphous emotions are localized and observable;
they have definite qualities. Emotions, like fluid objects,
are entities we observe. Images, memories, and thoughts
are objects we grasp, manipulate, and encompass by
awareness just as we do the components of the physical
world. In contrast, we cannot observe the observing self;
we must experience it directly. It has no defining qualities, no boundaries, no dimensions. The observing self has
been ignored by Western psychology because it is not an
object and cannot fit the assumptions and framework of
current theory.

Lacking understanding of this elusive, central self,
how are we to answer the essential questions "Who am
I?" "What am I?" that lie at the heart of science, philosophy, the arts, the search for meaning? To find answers
we must step outside the boundaries of our traditional
modes of thought.

Here too the mystical tradition has focused on an
area ignored by Western science. Both Yogic and Buddhist
metaphysics and psychology emphasize the crucial difference between the observer and the content of consciousness and use meditation techniques to heighten
the observing self. As with meaning, mystics hold that
answering "Who am I?" and "Why am I?" requires a special mode of perception. That claim is not surprising, considering the anomalous character of the observing self. To

understand the "I," we should first learn what the mystical tradition can teach us about it.

MOTIVATION AND CONSCIOUSNESS

A third area in which the mystical tradition can contribute to Western psychotherapy and Western culture is in the effect of motivation, or intention, on an individual's state of consciousness. Although modern psychotherapy is expressly concerned with motivational dynamics, it tends to address motives only when they produce conflict giving rise to symptoms. Yet there is considerable evidence that motivation is a major factor in the organization of consciousness. A person driving through rush-hour traffic to get to an appointment on time or relaxing after dinner and listening to music experiences in the two activities different modes of consciousness that are distinguished by different kinds of attention, acuteness of time sense, degree of self-object differentiation, and so on. This issue is important for psychotherapy because the state or mode of consciousness is the ground from which symptoms arise and largely determines the nature of those symptoms.

The mystical tradition has a sophisticated appreciation of the relation between basic motives, cognition, and perception. Much of the work of a mystical school focuses on exposing and changing motivations of its students as they express them in attitudes and everyday conduct. The need to change the mode of consciousness to develop a special perceptual capacity is seen in part as a need to lessen the intensity of motivations connected with the object self, the "ego." Although the mystical tradition is not a therapeutic system — the amelioration of symptoms is not its goal — symptoms often diminish as a by-product of its activities. An individual no longer dominated by motivations derived from the object self achieves a different perception and a different cognition, and symptoms belonging to the previous mode of consciousness tend to disappear. Although the disappearance of symptoms is a secondary effect in the context of mysticism, it is a primary goal for Western psychotherapy. Psychotherapists and patients alike stand to gain in their main purpose by attending to the mystical tradition's teachings about motivation and its relation to consciousness, issues that affect all aspects of their lives.

The problem of meaning, the observing self, and the effect of motivation on consciousness are all related. The enhancement of the observing self permits knowledge of one's motivations and the possibility for change. Change in motivation permits one to develop intuitive perception, which provides access to meaning. These vital areas and their interconnections are ones to which mysticism has paid special attention and about which it has gained special knowledge. Western psychology, were it to draw upon these insights, could achieve a larger understanding of human consciousness, which would not only increase the scope and effectiveness of psychotherapy but answer other needs even more important to our well-being.

For these reasons, we should consider what the mystical tradition can offer us, and explore its relevance not only for psychotherapy but for health and human development. If we do, I believe we can enter a new era of understanding that will clarify what we have thus far not been able to understand: the self. Our psychological theories are clumsy and inherently contradictory because we have misunderstood the observing center, the ground of our experience. As a result of disregarding the unique character, the transcendent nature of that observing self, contemporary psychology has been unable to free us from the confinement of our isolating and impoverishing assumptions.

For many years the voice in the night has been deaf to itself. It is time to listen.

Part I
THE LINKS

2

Mysticism as a Science

Westerners are likely to associate the mystical with a variety of alien images categorized as "spiritual" — bearded, robed gurus surrounded by worshipful devotees; delicate saints absorbed in ecstatic visions; ascetic hermits meditating in caves; beads, incense, whirling dances, vegetarian diets, chastity, chanting, and begging bowls.

These associations are far from the mark. Most "mystical teachings" with which we are familiar are the obsolete, displaced fragments of what were once complex, integrated systems of development adapted specifically to their diverse cultures. Practices that seem exotic to us were originally not exotic at all. Genuine mystical development requires forms appropriate to the people involved; it uses "the materials of the locality." Much of what we identify as "mystical" is a spurious carnival of deluded, misguided people and bizarre practices representing a hodgepodge of philosophies and techniques.

An old saying tells us that counterfeit coins are accepted only because real gold exists. We can begin to discern the gold contained in the mystical tradition by focusing our attention on its essentials and avoiding confusion due to its many different forms and the antiquated language of ancient texts. In so doing, we find a body of theory and techniques constituting a type of science, one closer to our own than we might imagine.

It may seem fanciful to call mysticism a science. After all, science is said to operate by a specific method consisting of three essential steps, apparently different from what is ordinarily considered to be mystical activity. These steps are (1) observing phenomena, (2) drawing conclusions from those observations, and (3) testing the conclusions against publicly observable, predicted consequences.

In fact, although the scientific method is generally accepted as an accurate model for the conduct of science, it does not generally account for the actual discovery of most great scientific truths, as has been documented by Michael Polanyi and others.[1] Dingle, a historian of science, summarizes the disparity between the standard scientific method and actual practice by stating that the former is

. . . a discipline conducted for the most part by logicians unacquainted with the practice of science, and it consists mainly of a set of principles by which accepted conclusions can best be reached by those who already know them. When we compare these principles with the steps by which the discoveries were actually made we find scarcely a single instance in which there is the slightest resemblance.[2]

The scientific method is employed for verification rather than for discovery, and verification lies at the heart of the seeming difference between mysticism and Western science. An insight that is not verifiable, some argue, lies outside the boundaries of science. For example, Bassui, a fourteenth-century Zen master, declared: "Your Mind-essence is not subject to birth or death. It is neither being nor nothingness, neither emptiness nor form-and-color."[3] What is a scientist to make of that? "Mind-essence" is not specifically defined and the statement cannot be verified by observation. Yet to answer that objection we might consider Einstein's assertion that space is "curved." Can we test that statement? We observe space and we observe curves, but our observations do not verify the assertion that space is curved. To our objections, Einstein might have replied, "The curvature of space is not perceptible through the five senses. If you will first study calculus and physics for a number of years, you will come to understand the truth of this statement and the way it relates to the phenomena with which you are familiar." Bassui would probably have given the same reply: " 'Mind-essence' is not something you can perceive with your five senses. If you will undertake certain special studies for a number of years, you will experience the truth of what I have said." Of course both Einstein and Bassui would also have added, "You will need a teacher who understands the subject, and appropriate material with which to work, and your attitude must be conducive to learning and you must have the intelligence and motivation needed to achieve comprehension in this difficult area." In this view, mysticism need not be considered alien to science.

Still, mysticism differs from science in its subject matter and the means it employs. One such difference is that mystics make personal data a major part of their work. Where Western science has looked outward at the world, mystics have turned their attention inward, to themselves, even to that which asks the questions. The mystic scientist becomes his own subject and his own consciousness is his data. Again, such an approach would seem to be quite unscientific, judging by the usual image of the scientist as a detached, objective recorder of publicly observable phenomena. That image, however, is more fantasy than reality. We know that observers are never detached in the sense of not influencing the subject of investigation. Einstein showed decisively that in measuring time and space the observer includes himself in the measurement; the scientist cannot only "observe." Heisenberg, in reviewing the subjective factor in science, noted:

> Looking back to the different concepts that have been formed in the past or may be formed in the future in the attempt to find our way through the world by means of science, we see that they appear to be ordered by the increasing part played by the subjective element in the set. Classical physics can be considered as the idealization in which we speak about the world as entirely separated from ourselves. [4]

Not only is the ideal of the objective observer theoretically impossible, and seldom achieved, but large areas of human experience require the investigator to be personally involved in the phenomena in question, since descriptions cannot convey them. For example, the experience of music, of making love, of swimming or dancing or the delights of fine food cannot be communicated by language — one must partake to understand what they are. In medicine, learning to diagnose illness is much the same. Only by listening repeatedly can one learn to distinguish the components of the heartbeat that seem so clearly distinguishable in the textbook. The need to experience personally the phenomena being investigated is best known in psychotherapy and psychoanalysis. It is generally agreed that students in these disciplines should themselves undergo psychotherapy or psychoanalysis during their training because, among other reasons, the reality of certain aspects of that experience cannot be communicated by words alone. Anyone who has first read about "transference" and later been caught up in that phenomenon realizes the difference between theory and experience. As with mystical consciousness, such subjects defy close description. They must be known by means of themselves.

Thus, Western science, including psychology, necessarily contains an important element of subjectivity and shares with mysticism the problem of limited access to its primary data through special training and information. However, more fundamental barriers are also involved.

The first barrier is the nature of language itself. Because we derive language from our experience with external objects, speech is inadequate for communicating such internal phenomena as feeling, and we cannot use it to establish a precise link between the internal events of two individuals. Traditionally, the arts have been used to communicate what descriptive language cannot, but the very lack of precision in the arts has placed them outside the category of science.

Just as research physicists, chemists, and biologists deliberately alter the materials or organisms they investigate, mystics employ procedures such as meditation to change students' consciousness and reveal new knowledge to them. Mystical consciousness involves a different perspective on time, causality, and self — a different reality, considered from our ordinary point of view. Applying everyday language to that special domain results in paradoxical statements for which the mystical literature is famous: "Raising the eyebrows is the mountain and ocean,"[5] or "It moves and moves not; it is far and likewise near."[6] Again, the difficulties of adapting everyday language to extraordinary experiences are not unknown to Western science, which must invent such words as *wavicle* to describe the paradoxical nature of light.

A second barrier limiting access to mystical experience is that mysticism is devoted to developing the capacity for intuitive knowing, a type of perception that bypasses the usual sensory channels and the rational intellect. (Ordinary intuition is said to be a faint echo of this capacity but not to be equated with it.) Thus, how can a teacher describe mystical perception to one who has not experienced it? A parable written by a contemporary Sufi illustrates the problem.

RADIOS

I was once in a certain country where the local people had never heard the sounds emitted from a radio receiver. A transistorized set was being brought to me; while waiting for it to arrive I tried to describe it to them. The general effect was that the description fascinated some and infuriated others. A minority became irrationally hostile about radios.

When I finally demonstrated the set, the people could not tell the difference between the voice from the loudspeaker and someone nearby. Finally, like us, they managed to develop the necessary discrimination of ear, such as we have.

And, when I had questioned them afterward, all swore that what they had imagined from descriptions of radios, however painstaking, did not correspond with the reality.[7]

These factors make it difficult for someone anchored in ordinary experience to assess the conclusions of mystical science. However, those who are willing to participate in that science can begin to establish a reference base in their own experience that will permit a mystic to communicate with them. By participating they can position themselves to make corroborating observations — that is, the phenomena of mystical experience become public to them. In the physical sciences, considerable intellectual, technical, and sensory training is necessary to the public understanding of certain observations. Similarly, those with the necessary mystical education have no trouble understanding each other and can share their observations, although such communication may be unintelligible to the untrained bystander. From a functional point of view, a specialist's knowledge is always private.

At the same time, one must realize that testing or validating mystical assertions is not as straightforward a process as it is in some areas of science. Galileo could drop two different weights for all to see and understand the results.

However, only one person at a time can directly observe the results of mystical investigation since it is carried on within the mystic, who serves as his or her own "control." Usually, only other mystics can perceive a change in the seeker and corroborate his or her findings through developed intuitive capacities. But remember, although experiments to confirm Einstein's theory of relativity permit public observation of the instrument readings, only a select, trained few can conduct such experiments and interpret the results. Thus, in this respect too, we find that mysticism is not as different from science as is usually assumed.

The mystical tradition is a discipline based on experience whose goal is knowledge of reality. Its subjectivity does not separate it from science, in which discovery also involves the subjective and nonrational. Both disciplines use reason but their insights into the basic nature of reality are based on intuitive processes. Because of this, modern Westerners can approach the mystical tradition without feeling they are betraying Western science or departing from its basic ground of observable experience. Similarly, psychotherapy and mysticism need not be at odds. In addition the history of psychotherapy reveals its roots in sacred healing rather than rational medicine; its practice is more an art than an exercise in logic or technique. These characteristics give it a kinship with the mystical tradition and the basis for learning from it. If prejudices and misconceptions about mysticism can be set aside, we will find that the mystical tradition contains a vital core of great importance to Western psychological science.

3

Psychotherapy as an Art

A principal barrier to the rapprochement of Western psychotherapy with the mystical tradition is the notion that mysticism is some kind of sloppy emotional state, at best a poetic operation, whereas Western psychotherapy is, or should be, the psychological kinsman and ally of objective science. On the contrary, mysticism, for all its appearance of irrationality, is based on a disciplined dedication to truth that makes it a science in the basic sense of that word, while psychotherapy retained its religious origins for centuries. For these reasons, psychotherapy is closer to the mystical tradition than to Western science. It is time for psychotherapy to become aware of its kinship with mysticism so that all may benefit from it.

In the early days of medicine, curing afflictions of unknown and mysterious origin — for example, hysterical possession, madness, acute sickness — fell into the domain of the medicine man, the shaman, and the priest. These early healers, who treated such conditions through exorcism and evoking the aid of spirits through magic, were the forebears of contemporary psychotherapists. By 700 B.C., when people believed that gods caused much human affliction, therapy was performed by priests, who offered sacrifices to the gods in appeasement, and by bards, who sang epic poems that validated the significance and meaning of human life.

In medieval Europe, madness was thought to be the result of demonic possession, as opposed to the classical Greek concept of possession by a god, but the priest was still responsible for treatment. During the Middle Ages medicine began to remove itself from theological control, but even by the seventeenth century, when this split was well defined, psychology and psychotherapy remained primarily the interest of philosophers and priests.

In philosophy, Leibniz provided a beginning concept of the unconscious, and Descartes discussed the childhood origin of adult perversions and preferences. In religion, Catholic priests were familiar with psychological problems expressed and dealt with in the confessional, and they wrote about sexual deviations. Most significant of all, Protestant ministers, while abolishing the formal ritual of confession, began to develop the Cure of the Soul, eliciting a pathogenic secret believed to lie at the heart of emotional distress.[1]

By the turn of the nineteenth century, however, medicine was firmly allied with rationalism, and the treatment of emotional and mental disorders became a specialty of medicine, not the church. Within that specialty a new split developed that reflected the same division of thought that had existed since earliest times.

One school believed that mental illness was biologically caused (brain dysfunction), the other in psychological causation. The brain-dysfunction theorists, the "organic" psychiatrists, continue to ally themselves with medicine and to emphasize drugs and somatic therapies. The psychogenic school, which inherited the mantle of philosophers and priests, is represented by psychotherapists of every persuasion. In its starkest form the psychogenic school is personified by the classical psychoanalyst, whose modus operandi is much closer to that of the priest in his confessional than of the physician in his or her treatment room.

Psychoanalysis, originated by Freud at the close of the nineteenth century, has provided the foundation for modern psychotherapy, and its principles have pervaded the general culture as well. It is significant that Freud, a physician, first attempted to develop a neurological theory of consciousness that would provide a suitable biological base for his theory of neurosis. He was initially delighted by this "Project for a Scientific Psychology" but abandoned it abruptly. In his preface to the work, Strachey comments:

> Nor is it hard to guess why. For he found that his neuronal machinery had no means of accounting for what, in *The Ego and the Id* he described as being "in the last resort our one beacon-light in the darkness of depth-psychology" — namely, "the property of being conscious or not."[2]

Freud never returned to a neurological model. He developed his clinical procedure, psychoanalysis, from hypnosis. The core of his approach was the Protestant Cure of Souls, although the religious connection was utterly severed and the concept of the "soul" abandoned.

Led by psychoanalysis, the psychotherapy of neurotic distress proceeded to develop on a line that veered farther and farther away from scientific medicine and toward psychology, philosophy, and metaphysics. Psychotherapy absorbed its technical procedures from psychoanalysis: the interpretation of resistance and transference, the understanding of adult behavior in terms of childhood experience, and the analysis of symptoms as adaptive strategies fall into the category of art because they are difficult, if not impossible, to measure, specifiable only within broad guidelines, and transmittable not through texts but through apprenticeship. A further indication of psychotherapy's artistic nature is the difficulty of assessing its results by focusing on technical and theoretical issues alone. To understand therapeutic outcomes it has become necessary to focus on less tangible qualities such as "warmth," "empathy," and "genuineness" and in these matters the relationships are complex.[3],[4] After reviewing these complexities, Mitchell and his colleagues concluded about the qualities important in a therapist:

> We want to emphasize the therapist-as-person before the therapist-as-expert or therapist-as-technician. We want to emphasize the commonality that psychotherapy has with the other aspects of life. *We want to emphasize the therapist as a viable human being engaged in a terribly human endeavor.*[5]

Psychotherapy can be very effective, but its effectiveness is not a matter of theoretical persuasion or the application of a special technique. It appears to depend on an appropriate match of therapist and patient; on therapist skills such as empathy, self-knowledge, and attentiveness; and on a training system, based on supervision by senior therapists, that helps students acquire the "tacit knowledge" of someone who has learned clinical wisdom.[6] "Books can tell you what to do, but not when to do it."

Although psychotherapy is more an art than scientific medicine, many of the qualities inherent in effective psychotherapy are essential to good physicians who address the psychological dimensions of their patients and thus are able to practice the "art" of medicine. But though the differences in approach between psychotherapy and scientific medicine are subtle, they do separate each discipline from the other. Ellenberger's distinctions between Primitive Healing and Scientific Therapy are useful in appreciating the difference between the psychotherapeutic and the orthodox medical approach. One need only substitute "Psychotherapy" for the left-hand column head below and "Scientific Medicine" for the right-hand one.

Primitive Healing	Scientific Therapy
1. The healer is much more than a physician; he is the foremost personality of his social group.	1. The therapist is a specialist among many others.
2. The healer exerts his action primarily through his personality.	2. The therapist applies scientific techniques in an impersonal way.
3. The healer is preponderantly a psychosomatician; he treats many physical diseases by psychological techniques.	3. There is a dichotomy between physical and psychic therapy. The accent in psychiatry is on the physical treatment of mental illness.
4. The healer's training is long and exacting, and often includes the experience of a severe emotional disease that he has to overcome in order to be able to heal other people.	4. The training is purely rational and does not take into consideration the personal, medical, or emotional problems of the physician.
5. The healer belongs to a school of its own teachings and traditions diverging from those of other schools.	5. The therapist acts on the basis of a unified medicine, which is a branch of science and is not esoteric teachings.[7]

"Primitive healing" and psychotherapy, then, address the psychological aspects of human life just as "scientific therapy" addresses the physical. The former category is necessarily more subjective than the latter. Because of the psychological dimensions involved the primitive healer and the modern psychotherapist must employ a different mode of knowing than the scientist who focuses on objects and physical effects. This mode might be called *participatory knowing* — knowing the psychological and physiological world of another by experiencing our equivalent of it. We are not aware of how much this subjective understanding operates in our everyday lives, let alone in the psychotherapeutic situation. For example, when listening to someone talk, we are far more intimately involved with the speaker than we realize. Condon subjected films of conversation to "microanalysis," in which he studied, frame-by-frame, the minute physical movements of the speaker and the listener and found them to match precisely with microunits of speech. For example, the syllable *ae* lasted 3/48 second and was accompanied by specific patterns of movement of the head, fingers, mouth, and shoulder. This was a striking finding, but even more startling was an additional phenomenon:

> Listeners were observed to move in precise shared synchrony with the speaker's speech. This appearas to be a form of entrainment since there is no discernible lag, even at 1/48 second. This has been called interactional synchrony. It also appears to be a universal characteristic of human communication, and perhaps characterizes much of animal behavior in general. Communication is thus like a dance, with everyone engaged in intricate and shared movements across many shared movements across many subtle dimensions, yet all strangely oblivious that they are doing so.[8]

If this takes place in ordinary conversation, participatory knowing must take place to an even greater degree in the psychotherapeutic situation in which the therapist is the active listener par excellence, actually quite different from the detached, analytic observer that is the ideal of Western science.

Emotional communication is even more participatory than verbal interchange. We understand another's emotions through empathy or identification, realizing that we know the other person's emotion by experiencing a similar feeling. In contrast, the physician dealing with a patient's physical state by measuring white blood corpuscles, excising a tumor, or deducing the effects of a drug employs objective observation, logic, and facts. Thus the psychological and the physical domain call for different modes of knowing. When body processes must be assessed, empirical observation and laboratory data can be employed, but the assessment of psychological processes may require that therapists employ their own emotional responses to detect the state of the patient. For example, a therapist who responds to a patient with feelings of boredom, anger, sexual desire, enhanced self-esteem, or fear during a session can gain through those feelings information about the patient's activities and feelings, information that is usually more reliable than that conveyed by words or facial cues.

Students training to be therapists are taught to use themselves as measuring instruments. Such subjectivity, the essence of art, is antithetical to rational science. While the Western scientist has striven to be objective, guided solely by empirical observations, independent of emotions and wishes, therapists learn to view their emotions and impulses as data available to them. Thus, while modern psychotherapists employ their scientific knowledge of psychodynamics, they practice an art, as did their early predecessors. For this reason, psychiatrists who are psychotherapists exclusively are hard put to justify their work as part of the practice of medicine. There may come a time when we understand that all of medicine should encompass the modes of knowing employed in both art and science, but at present the division between psychotherapy and scientific medicine is significant and must be appreciated.

It is important for psychiatrists, and psychotherapists in general, to understand the different origins of psychotherapy, on the one hand, and organic psychiatry and medicine, on the other, and not feel they must align themselves with the world view of the physical sciences. For just as did peoples of ancient times, we too must deal with the problem of attaining meaningful, happy lives in the face of uncertainty, disaster, old age, and death. Unlike the ancients, we turn to psychology and formal psychotherapy for help, for the priest and the philosopher are no longer able to answer those problems manifested in a modern context. However, psychologists and psychotherapists bound by the metaphysical assumptions of modern science also fail to help us. An approach is needed suitable to the intangible dimensions of human experience. Such an approach will inevitably be closer to art than to rational science insofar as it requires an intuitive orientation and a respect for the nonrational as well as the rational. Contemporary psychodynamic theory need not be discarded but one must be willing to go beyond the definition of reality given by science and be open to possibilities better communicated by the arts than by mathematics. That attitude, coupled with the understanding that Western psychotherapy stems from the tradition of sacred healing and is related to it in its mode of operation, should make it possible to turn to the mystical tradition for aid in dealing with the existential problems that modern psychotherapy has been unable to solve.

4

The Origins of Mysticism

To learn the basic principles of mysticism and to dispel the misconceptions and prejudices that obscure our understanding, we must turn to the classical texts of mysticism. By so doing we discover a fundamental unanimity underlying the diverse traditions of this science. Over and over again, we encounter similar principles and procedures for achieving a special understanding of reality. This basic agreement should arouse the curiosity of even the most skeptical reader and give credence to the argument that the mystical tradition is not dealing with fantasies or delusions but with something real. The idea that mysticism is relevant to psychotherapy becomes quite plausible when it becomes apparent that mystical procedures are often aimed at changing automatic patterns of perception and thinking, the source of much human suffering. If the mystics are correct, Western psychotherapists cannot afford to ignore these teachings that have persisted through the centuries in all parts of the world.

Let us now take up the mystical texts themselves to clarify the basic tenets of mysticism and to demonstrate their simultaneous origin in a number of different cultures.

VEDANTA

No one can say when mysticism began. The earliest recorded tradition, the Vedic literature of India, is thought to have been composed anywhere from five thousand to three thousand years ago, but it was not written down until relatively recently. Although mystical activity may well have occurred in earlier cultures, the most ancient human records are in hieroglyphics or cuneiform, writings that contain little practical advice. So we must begin with India.

The Indian Vedic literature is composed of four sections: the Rig Veda, the Brahmanas, the Aranyakas, and the Upanishads, which are distinctive from the rest of the Vedic material and were composed later, from 900 B.C. onward.

[The Upanishads] represent free and bold attempts to find out the truth without any thought of a system. Notwithstanding the variety of authorship and the period of time covered by them, we discern in them a unity of purpose and a vivid sense of spiritual reality. They are distinguished from the Vedic hymns and the Brahmanas by their increased emphasis on monistic suggestions and subjective analysis, as well as their indifference to Vedic authority and ceremonial piety.[1]

The Upanishads teach that the way to relieve the suffering of life is to go beyond the categories of thought to experience the reality that underlies everything, the Real Self of each person. As Stace and others have pointed out, the basic mystical experience is that of an undifferentiated unity, interpreted by the Upanishads as (1) the Real Self of the individual, and (2) the Real Self as the Ultimate that lies beyond and within all reality, mental and physical. Thus, in the Chandogya Upanishad, Uddalaka informs his son about the nature of Brahma (Reality):

He is the truth. He is the subtle essence of all. He is the Self. And that, Svetaku, THAT ART THOU.[2]

This statement, in different forms, occurs throughout the mystical literature of later centuries.

The phrase *undifferentiated unity* can be spoken easily

and quickly, but most people do not know what it means. According to mystics, it is an experience in which the unusual division between self and the world of objects ceases to exist. The experience is one of supreme bliss, of ultimate fulfillment, but one does not experience it as one would eating an ice cream cone. The person is no longer separated from the experience; the person becomes the experience. Most important of all, undifferentiated unity is not sensory, not a super orgasm; one reaches the experience intuitively. The pure state is temporary, but one who has known it can expand his or her comprehension of life and undergo a personality transformation.

That Art Thou was not easily perceived by the people of India. The Upanishads themselves are subject to different interpretations, from one of Unity to the more traditional dualism of man and God. Dualism gains the ascendancy as mysticism is taught to those without previous mystical experience as their vantage point. Mystical assertions of basic Unity — no matter how much bliss they promise — are not sufficiently compelling to overcome the ordinary experience of individuality, the distinction between the self and the world of everyday consciousness. It is as if the mystical intuition of Unity and the everyday sense of the separate self were two magnetic poles whose opposing pulls create a spectrum of intermediate philosophies to fill the space between them. The reality intuited by the mystic is convincing only when it is experienced; people who lack that experience adapt the concept to the world of the senses.

Thus we find that by the sixth century B.C., the teaching of the Upanishads — *That Art Thou* — had become obscured by the growth of Brahmanic ritual and sacrificial ceremonies in the service of the Hindu gods. The social caste system had been adopted to form a religion in which the priests (Brahmins) were at the top, and the gods of the early

Vedic literature were worshiped as independent, dualistic entities. This formalism inspired a number or protests, one of which was led by Siddhartha Guatama, son of a warrior king, who had renounced the worldly life to study and practice austerities under a variety of religious teachers. Siddhartha finally abandoned all worldly traditions and attained "the realization of the Ultimate." His name, Buddha, means "The Enlightened One."

Buddha described a reality devoid of God, gods, or soul. The principal thrust of his teaching was that the ordinary experience of an individual self or a soul is an illusion. Suffering, which arises from that illusion, is cured by the realization of the truth. However, Buddha stressed that his teaching was a Way, not a philosophy, and he refused to answer such questions as, "Is the universe eternal or not?" He declared that his Way led to the realization of ultimate reality, which he termed *Nirvana*. As in the Upanishads, and in mystical literature in general, the Ultimate was defined by Buddha in negatives. Nirvana, or the Absolute, is "the extinction of illusion; . . . the unborn, ungrown, and unconditioned."[3] Nirvana is beyond the ordinary categories of thought and experience.

In addition, Buddha's teaching innovatively stressed the necessity of ethical behavior. He taught noninjury, forgiveness of enemies, and friendliness as an essential part of his Way. He made motivation a criterion for judging a person's actions, whereas in the Hinduism of his time the goodness of a person was assessed in terms of conformity to ceremonial acts or rituals, or by the totality of overtly good or bad acts performed.

According to Buddhist texts, the principal technical means for attaining enlightenment is "concentration" or meditation, a procedure that begins with fixing the mind or attention on a sensory stimulus and progresses to a point of alert receptiveness, of pure mindfulness. Finally, the meditator goes beyond the apprehension of senses, thoughts, and feelings to a cessation of all faculties — an unnamable Void. Only by achieving moral discipline and extinguishing the idea of self can an individual realize fully the Nirvana that comes through concentration.

Buddhism spread rapidly over India, into Burma, Ceylon, China, and eventually Japan, merging with Taoism to produce Chinese and Japanese Zen. An enormous body of scriptures was recorded and many schisms arose, resulting in a spectrum of philosophies similar to that developed in India from various interpretations of Vedanta. Eventually, Buddha, who had preached a world without self, God, or gods, was subjected by a variety of schools to interpretations ranging from the original doctrine of not-self to the doctrine of the Pudgalavadins. They postulated a soullike *pudgala* that persists through several lives until it attains Nirvana. The statues of a multitude of Buddhas and Bodhisattvas found in Buddhist temples give testimony to the fact that while Nirvana may have been enough for the monks, the laity required many different Buddhas to whom they could pray and look for beneficience. It is interesting that the Buddhist literature itself prophesied an inevitable decline from the first vigorous phase to later phases in which the attainment of enlightenment would become all but impossible.

THE GREEK PHILOSOPHERS

During this same period a similar current began to flow from Greece. Paramenides (about 500–450 B.C.) taught that Being had no beginning and no end, that it was changeless and infinite and without parts. He said that God was Truth and Reason, and existed within the human mind. After him,

Plato (427?–347 B.C.) instructed that Reason and Truth were immortal and that the soul should free itself from Matter by contemplation of the beautiful. He depicted the human race as being imprisoned in a cave, mistaking shadows for reality. When persons are able to free themselves they can leave the cave and find the source of shadows and of light:

> Socrates: And with that he will discover that it is the sun which gives the seasons and the years, and is the chief in the field of the things which are seen, and in some ways the cause even of all the things he had been seeing before. If he now went back in his mind to where he was living before, and to what his brother slaves took to be wisdom there, wouldn't he be happy at the change and pity them?
> Glaucon: Certainly, he would.[4]

The same basic propositions that were put forth at about the same time in the Upanishads, in the Buddhist sutras, and by the Greek philosophers — roughly between 500 and 350 B.C. — are found as well in the Taoist writings of Lao Tzu and in the Wisdom Books of the Old Testament, believed to date from the same period. This simultaneity among disparate cultures is quite startling. No explanation seems adequate that does not concede some basis in reality for these mystical assertions.

SUFISM

During the Middle Ages, the last widespread articulation of mysticism, Sufism, developed in the Middle East. I will pay particular attention to Sufism, for its expression is more contemporary to our own culture than any of the traditions discussed thus far. Sufism is often said to have originated with Mohammed, but long before him there were people referred to as "The Near Ones," "The People of Truth," "The Masters." The word *Sufi* was applied to them later, and the word *Sufism* did not appear until the nineteenth century, when it was coined by a German scholar.

More clearly and emphatically than any mystics before them, the Sufis stressed that all religious forms were cultural derivations of the same basic intuitive perception. For example, Ibn el-Arabi states:

MY HEART CAN TAKE ON ANY APPEARANCE

My heart can take on any appearance. The heart varies in accordance with variations of the innermost consciousness. It may appear in form as a gazelle meadow, a monkish cloister, an idol-temple, a pilgrim Kaaba, the tablets of the Torah for certain sciences, the bequest of the leaves of the Koran.[5]

As did the sages of earlier traditions, the Sufis asserted that a suprasensory reality existed that could be known by human beings. Such knowledge revealed the meaning of human life and its flow of events. The Sufis made the particular point that most people are "asleep," because their consciousness is taken up with automatic responses in the service of greed and fear. The brain, thus occupied, is said to be incapable of the special perception whose development is the true destiny and task of human life. Thus, "the secret protects itself." According to the Sufis, the human race can undergo "conscious evolution" by freeing itself from its conditioned assumptions and self-centered thinking.

The first task of students of the Sufis' science is not to immerse themselves in asceticism, meditation, or other traditional practices, but to "learn how to learn," and teaching stories were developed for that purpose. Although such stories are found in earlier traditions as well, the Sufis seem to have made particularly extensive use of this device and regard it as a potent means of preparing the student's mind for further study. The function of teaching stories is to reveal the socially sanctioned patterns and motives in behavior of which the student is unaware.

According to the Sufis, "awakening" is the primary task of human life, our evolutionary destiny. Rumi states:

THIS TASK

You have a duty to perform. Do anything else, do any number of things, occupy your time fully, and yet, if you do not do this task, all your time will have been wasted.[6]

HOW FAR YOU HAVE COME!

Originally, you were clay. From being mineral, you became vegetable. From vegetable, you became animal, and from animal, man. During these periods man did not know where he was going, but he was being taken on a long journey nonetheless. And you have to go through a hundred different worlds yet.[7]

The emphasis here on "conscious evolution" is more prominent than in the literature of earlier traditions. The Hindu and Buddhist texts spoke of endlessly repeating cycles, the "dance" of Krishna, or the unchanging reality of Nirvana underlying the empty "shadows" at our perception. Nevertheless, an evolutionary theme is implied in the Buddhist vow "to save all sentient beings," and the hierarchy of gods in Indian mythology can be viewed as an allegory of that development.

The Sufis define "spiritual growth" as the development of a latent intuitive capacity present in all human beings. They use the metaphor of a blind man who is taught to develop sight by a science that makes little sense to him until he achieves the experience of vision. Such a science, they say, must be individualized, shaped to match the specific time, place, and person in question. When it is, a suitably motivated and equipped candidate becomes able to perceive directly the reality underlying the world of appearances. However, antiquated systems and their fragments, which are often preserved and venerated, are useless for attaining that goal. With considerable sophistication, the Sufi literature details the manner in which once-viable teaching systems inevitably become automatized and perverted to serve social and emotional needs. Only a Teacher, someone who has attained "sight," can select from any individual's environment and from the repertoire of available techniques a curriculum suitable to the task. For this reason, the Sufis say, an active school of mystical science is often invisible to those who expect the traditional.

The Sufis' focus on a special type of perception is not unique. A similar theme is implied in all mystical literature that refers to the experience of suprasensory perception, beyond concepts and sensations. However, the Sufis are much more specific in their description of the problems involved in achieving that perception, and their psychological analysis shows a quite modern approach to motivational issues. The Sufis' emphasis on evolution, on adapting one Teaching to different cultures, on the problems of conditioned thinking, and on the subtleties of behavior and motivation makes their writings particularly interesting to students of our own psychologically oriented culture.

THE SCIENCE OF INTUITIVE DEVELOPMENT

With these texts in mind, we can think of the entire history of mysticism as the history of a science of intuitive development. This science takes various forms according to the country in which it is at work, it gives rise to religions but is independent of them, and it is based on practical considerations of human psychology. Its goal is understanding the reality that underlies the world of ordinary experience.

Unlike the physical sciences, which rely primarily on rational, analytic skills applied to information processed by the sensory organs, mysticism relies on direct, intuitive perception. The special strategies and technology of mysticism aim to awaken the intuitive capacity of its students. Once awakening takes place, students can proceed on their own, independent of the teaching system that developed their knowledge.

According to mystics, the fundamental reality underlying appearances is not accessible to the senses. It cannot be described in terms derived from the ordinary world, but it is accessible to mystical intuition. The perception of that underlying reality gives meaning to individual existence and does away with the fear of death and the self-centered desires that direct the lives of most people. The intuition of the nature of reality marks the transition to the next stage of evolutionary development, which is the destiny of the human race. The end of that process cannot be seen.

This overview and summary of mysticism makes it obvious that Western psychotherapy cannot enrich itself through the mystical tradition without studying mysticism on its own terms. It is not necessary to set aside the accomplishments of our own science. To the contrary, our knowledge of psychological development is helpful and necessary to understanding the logic and purpose behind the methods of mystical science.

5

Intuition

Mystical science is based on the possibility of direct knowledge of basic reality — a capacity for knowing akin to what we term *intuition.* If no such capacity exists, if the senses and ordinary intellect are our only sources of knowledge of the world and of ourselves, then mysticism is a false and foolish venture. And so it has been judged by most modern psychologists, psychiatrists, and physical scientists. Yet the hypothesis of mystical intuition is legitimate in terms of our own science. The technical procedures of mysticism that appear so strange and impractical can be understood as necessary and logical means for bringing about the development of the intuitive capacity.

The concept of intuition has never been admitted into psychiatry's formal view of the human psyche. As an illustration of that fact, compare the following metaphors, the first drawn from Freud and the second from Sufi literature. Freud likened the human being to a rider on a horse:

> The ego's relation to the id might be compared with that of a rider to his horse. The horse supplies the locomotive energy, while the rider has the privilege of deciding on the goal and of guiding the powerful animal's movements.[1]

In this view, reason is in charge. But in the Sufi metaphor of the chariot, the rider of the chariot is intuition:

Picture a charioteer. He is seated in a vehicle, pro-
pelled by a horse, guided by himself. Intellect is
the "vehicle," the outward form within which we
state where we think we are and what we have to
do. This is what we call *tashkil*, outward shape or
formulation. The horse, which is the motive power,
is the energy, which is called "a state of emotion"
or other force. This is needed to propel the chariot.
The man, in our illustration, is that which perceives,
in a manner superior to others, the purpose and
possibilities of the situation, and who makes it possible for the chariot to move towards and to gain
its objective.[2]

For Freud, as for most contemporary psychologists and philosophers, the "man" is reason. For mystics, the "man" is intuition. The distinction reflects the basic difference between
Western scientific empiricism and mystical science.

Western psychotherapy, in basing itself almost exclusively on the world view of scientific materialism, has im-
poverished its model of human consciousness and lost the
meaning and significance of human life. For this reason alone,
the need to affirm the function of intuition is especially important because our intimations of a larger existence ordinarily find no support from our scientific culture but, instead,
opposition. That issue is addressed by the quotation in the
frontispiece: "A voice whispered to me last night: 'There is
no such thing as a voice whispering in the night!' " We can accept the reality of that voice without discarding the gains of
science. We can extend our science to a new domain.

DEFINING INTUITION

Mystical science asserts that human beings have an inherent capacity for knowing the meaning of their lives and
the nature of their real selves. That knowing is direct —

"intuitive" — not mediated by reason* or the sensory organs. The word *intuition* has its roots in the Latin *intueri*: to look at or toward, to contemplate. A typical dictionary definition of the word reads, "the act or faculty of knowing without the use of rational processes: immediate cognition."[4] The term *intuition* has been used to describe any process of acquiring knowledge that differs from conscious thought and bypasses the senses and memory. Thus, hunches, sudden solutions to problems, "feeling" the right choice in a dilemma, scientific creativity, the axioms of geometry, and receiving the ineffable "knowledge" that mysticism seeks to have all been termed *intuition*. Accordingly, many different explanations of intuition have been offered, and the true meaning of the term as used in the mystical tradition has been clouded.

The basic concept of intuition is ancient. Throughout history, human beings have had the experience of knowing more than what was given them by their senses. They have attributed such unexplained knowledge either to divine intervention, as in the case of prophecy, or to a special quasi-magical ability possessed by only a few individuals, such as clairvoyants or great scientists. This "gift" was long considered to be the property of gods or spirits, not the heritage of ordinary men and women. Few people considered the possibility that such sporadic instances of intuition might be lower-order manifestations of a capacity that could be developed until it became a reliable channel of knowing.

The existence of such a channel, operating outside the intellect and sensory pathways, seems impossible to Western science, because there is no place in its cosmology or

*Although *reason* has a variety of meanings, especially in philosophy, the word will be used here to mean "the intellectual process of seeking truth or knowledge by inferring from either fact or logic."[3]

psychology for any means of knowing other than rationality or sensation. We cannot imagine any other process at work. Indeed, because we have achieved vast control and understanding of the physical and biological domains we have not been motivated to challenge scientific rationalism or to look for other avenues of knowledge. After all, what else is there? The answer to that question is intuition.

A HISTORY OF THE IDEA

"We are led to the concept of intuition by awareness of concepts not given in sensory experience — we know more than we should."[5]

For thousands of years, thinkers have attempted to grapple with the issue of our knowing more than we should and have used the term *intuition* in different ways, each reflecting particular theories of knowledge based on the assumptions of specific cultures. A brief historical overview of the concept of intuition will reveal the origins of the multiple meanings now attached to the term and the implications of those meanings for one's view of human consciousness.

In Plato's *Meno,* Socrates declares:

> The soul, then, as being immortal, and having been born again many times, and having seen all things that exist, whether in this world or in the world below, has knowledge of them all; and it is no wonder that she would be able to call to remembrance all that she ever knew . . . for all inquiry and all learning is but recollection.[6]

Remembrance has been called intuition because it does not result from the use of the intellect or the senses; rather, it is a recollection: we already know and therefore *recognize* the truth. Strictly speaking, Plato's concept is not precisely the same as the intuition of mystical science, which is a perception at a higher level than that of geometric truth or the "good" of popular consensus. Furthermore, mystical intuition is developed; it is not given. However, Plato may have intended this description to serve as a teaching device for communicating a similar concept, since in other passages, especially in the cave metaphor of *The Republic*, he indicates the need to free oneself from preoccupation with the world of appearances in order to see clearly. The prisoners in the cave cannot immediately confront the sun but must progress by degrees to that capacity:

> . . . the natural power to learn lives in the soul and is like an eye which might not be turned from the dark to the light without turning round of the whole body. The instrument of knowledge has to be turned around to the things of being, till the soul is able, by degrees, to support the light of true being and can look at the brightest.[7]

Thus, by a power higher than the senses or ordinary reason, human beings can perceive a certain and permanent truth — provided their attention is no longer fixed upon the shadows.

Plato's vision finds a striking parallel in the legends of the Hopi people, whose cultural roots go back as far as those of the Greeks. The Hopi tradition speaks of a fall from grace in which human beings experience themselves as progressively more separate from earth, animals, and other humans. The return to grace is through reunion. The cause of the fall is ascribed to people's forgetting their true nature and purpose. According to the Hopis, a psychophysical vibratory center responsive to the Great Spirit exists in the top of the head to serve as a guide — it "sees" what other senses do not. Persons with "the door open" have not forgotten their relationship to the divine and continue to praise it. They are saved in each epoch because they can hear the instructions of the Spirit.[8]

Why do the Hopi myths parallel Plato? Although Plato has been interpreted in different ways, from the perspective

of mystical science he teaches that basic truth is arrived at intuitively, not logically. His dialogues are not intended to
"prove" anything; rather, they communicate a perception
similar to that of the mystics, which is not the property or
creation of any one culture or epoch. For both Greeks and
Hopis, the deep perception of the human situation was similar. The special "insight" mentioned in their teachings is
gained neither through the senses nor through reason; it is intuitive and transcends culture and time.

Spinoza's definition of intuition is closest of all the
philosophers' to that of mystical science. Writing in the seventeenth century, Spinoza distinguished between knowledge
derived from the sense perception and careful reasoning about
observed phenomena ("opinion" and "reason") and the highest stage of human knowledge, in which the whole of the universe is comprehended as a unified interconnected system.
This highest knowledge he termed intuition, something that
grows out of empirical and scientific knowledge but rises
above them. In essence, it is knowledge of God. To Spinoza,
God exists in different "manifestations," all of which are part
of the same unified system operating in harmony. Rationality
provides a broader scope for intuition but it cannot show us
what intuition can.[9]

Kant proposed that space and time, as commonly con-
ceived, are, like the fundamental axioms of geometry, ab-
solutely true and exist as "categorical imperatives," prior to
logical thought or sensation. He regarded these concepts as
the products of "pure intuition."*

Unfortunately for Kant's philosophy, modern mathematics and physics have demonstrated that the fundamental

---

*Bertrand Russell points out that "intuition" is a poor translation of *Anschauung*,
which means "looking at" or "view." Space and time, according to Kant, are
a priori in the sense of being part of the apparatus of perception; they did not
imply to him the existence of another mode or channel of knowledge.[10]

axioms of geometry, thought for centuries to be irrefutable, are only relatively true, depending entirely on the frame of reference employed. Ordinary concepts of space and time are found to be matters of habit based on early learning. In a similar vein, Richard Von Mises cites Gonseth: "The . . . rules of logic and common sense are nothing else than an abstract schema drawn from the world of concrete objects."[11]

Less abstractly, Von Senden's studies of the congenitally blind who later acquire sight, to be discussed in Chapter 5, indicate why "space" can be a fallible concept: it is learned, not given. Reports suggest that human beings develop the experience of space through practice in looking at objects. The "intuition" of space is most likely a posteriori, not a priori. According to mystics, intuitive truth is usually of a higher order than what can be expressed in simple object world concepts, such as geometric axioms. Thus, Kant's "intuition" is closer to what contemporary philosophers call "implicit inference" than to intuition as defined by the mystics. The thinking process used to arrive at the concepts Kant calls intuitive goes on outside awareness but is not different from conscious thought or learning.

Two hundred and fifty years after Kant, at the beginning of the twentieth century, Henri Bergson emphasized the importance of employing intuition rather than relying exclusively on the intellect or "analysis":

> . . . philosophers agree in making a deep distinction between two ways of knowing a thing. The first implies going all around it, the second entering into it. The first depends on the viewpoint chosen and the symbols employed, while the second is taken from no viewpoint and rests on no symbols. Of the first kind of knowledge, we shall say that it stops at the relative; of the second that, wherever possible, it attains the absolute . . . an absolute can only be given in an intuition, while all the rest has to do with analysis. We call intuition here the sympathy by which one is transported

into the interior of an object in order to coincide with what
there is unique and consequently inexpressible in it.[12]

Bergson's point of view is quite close to that of mystical
science in his emphasis on intuition as direct (absolute)
knowing.

In modern times, however, the "intuitionism" of the
philosophers, whatever its form, has been largely replaced by
logical positivism, which assumes that all knowledge comes
from reasoning about sensory information. Any knowledge
labeled "intuitive" is believed to originate from the reasoning
processes outside awareness. The "intuitor" is unaware of the
steps or the inferences he or she actually employs and thus
mistakenly believes a nonsensory and nonrational process
has taken place. This reduces intuition to unconscious inference, an interpretation that dominates current philosophy,
psychiatric thinking, and almost all contemporary psychological theory and research.

In fact, modern psychiatry has never paid much attention to intuition in the classical sense of that term. In 1932,
in his *New Introductory Lectures*, Freud declared with confidence that ". . . no new source of knowledge or methods of
research have come into being. Intuition, and divination would
be such, if they existed; but they may safely be reckoned as
illusions, the fulfillment of wishful impulses."[13] This view
persists among contemporary psychoanalysts, who classify
intuition as either empathy (a process of emotional identification), imagination, or creativity ("regression in the service
of ego").[14, 15]

Some people think Carl Jung was attuned to the mystical. It is easy to assume that he used *intuition* to refer to
the same process as the one that concerns mystical science,
but this is not so. Rather, he used *intuition* to refer to a
basic personality capacity: "But intuition, as I conceive it, is

one of the basic functions of the psyche; namely, *perception of the possibilities inherent in a situation.*"[16] Jung considered intuition to be an unconscious process whose primary function "is simply to transmit images, or perceptions or relations between things, which could not be transmitted by other functions, or only in a very roundabout way."[17] Thus, intuition perceives the relationship of entities. However, Jung's position was closer to Freud's than to mysticism's, for his "intuition" is another function, like thinking, sensation, and feeling, that can be right or wrong — it is not direct knowing.*

Similarly, contemporary psychoanalytic theory and the general literature of psychiatry do not recognize intuition as being qualitatively different from functions with which we are familiar.

Jerome Bruner expressed the view of the majority of psychologists that intuitive discoveries are the result of free combinations of the elements of a problem:

> Intuition implies the art of grasping the meaning or significance or structure of a problem without explicit reliance on the analytic apparatus of one's craft . . . It is founded on a kind of combinatorial playfulness.[18]

Such a view comes largely from restricting the investigation of intuition to the type of isolated "problem" that lends itself to controlled psychological experiment. Unfortunately, Bruner applies the conclusions derived from this limited domain to a much broader field of human experience, as if the two were identical. As a result, the term he uses to denote the capacity to solve a geometric puzzle is the same as that for the capacity to perceive the meaning of life, and he jams both together into the same mechanical box.

---

*Although one would expect that Jung was familiar with the mystical definition of intuition, it is hard to find any clear statement about it in his writing.

In fairness to Bruner, he recognized that intuition was not just a matter of running through all the possible permutations of the elements of a problem like a super computer, and that discernment or choice is exercised among those few combinations that are useful:

> To create consists precisely in not making useless combinations and in making those which are useful and which are only a small minority. Invention is discernment, choice. If not a brute algorithm, then it must be a heuristic that guides us to a fruitful combination. What is the heuristic?[19]

That Bruner cannot specify.

In reviewing the history of the concept of intuition, we can see that intuition was first considered to be a special kind of contact with ultimate reality. The view later shifted to intuition as a perception of rather limited basic truths in the same category as principles of deductive logic, mathematical axioms, the idea of casuality, and the like. Finally, the dominant view today is that intuition is merely unconscious inference. The concept of a special capacity for suprasensory, direct knowing is rejected, as is the concept of truth itself. Westcott summarizes the current notion:

> Truth is to be understood as either a set of conventions or a set of probability statements, both subject to change. Immediate evidence (intuition) is seen as a result of insufficient analysis or inferential processes.[20]

In this latter view, the consequences of intuition have no more intrinsic value than those of reason and sensation.*

THE ANALOGY IN SCIENTIFIC DISCOVERY

The basic problem for philosophers, psychologists, and everyone else is that they cannot be convinced of the reality of something they have not experienced. So those who define

---

*Recently, there has been more recognition of intuition as a mode of knowing; see Vaughan.[21]

intuition as implicit inference are probably referring, correctly, to that type of "intuition" with which they are familiar. Certain forms of problem solving, "hunches," and "feelings" undoubtedly fall within the purview of Freud's or Bruner's view and also constitute the "implicit inference" of logical positivists. However, the intuition that Plato, Spinoza, Bergson, and the mystics refer to is an experience different from the lesser events ordinarily labeled "intuition." In contrast to "hunches," mystics say, their "sight" clarifies the nature of the self, the meaning of the flow of events, and the purpose of life. At the same time, mystical intuition can be applied to the domains of physical science and psychology — as evidenced by the *Maha yana* sutras and the writings of Lao Tse, Dogen, El Ghazali, and Shabastari. The unanimity of mystics' descriptions of intuited reality indicates that their experience is not idiosyncratic but universal, and the parallel between their descriptions and the discoveries of modern physics supports the validity of the universal view. Indeed, a Westerner can gain some appreciation of the reality of mystical intuition through the study of parallels between mystical insights of centuries ago and the view of reality currently being constructed by physicists. Such comparisons have been made by LeShan,[22] Capra,[23] and Zukov.[24]

It is ironic that academic psychology, which has tried to model itself after the physical sciences, dismisses intuition except as unconscious reasoning or inference, while physical scientists are much readier to acknowledge intuition as a process that is fundamentally different from, and superior to, reason, in discovering truth. Wigner, a Nobel physicist, commented:

The discovery of the laws of nature requires first and foremost intuition, conceiving of pictures and a great many subconscious processes. The use and also the confirmation of these laws is another matter... logic comes after intuition.[25]

And Gauss, the famous mathematician was, in the common view, describing the dilemma that arises from this reversal of the scientific method when he said, "I have had my solutions for a long time, but I do not yet know how I am to arrive at them."[26]

The most extensive and detailed survey of the process of scientific discovery was made by Michael Polanyi, who studied scientists' own descriptions of how they arrived at their "breakthroughs" to a new view of reality. Like Wigner, he found that logic, data, and reasoning came last — they first used another channel of knowing. There was no word for that channel in ordinary vocabulary, so Polanyi used an analogy to convey its nature:

> And we know that the scientist produces problems, has hunches, and, elated by these anticipations, pursues the quest that should fulfill these anticipations. This quest is guided throughout by feelings of a deepening coherence and these feelings have a fair chance of proving right. We may recognize here the powers of a dynamic intuition. The mechanism of this power can be illuminated by an analogy.
>
> Physics speaks of potential energy that is released when a weight slides down a slope. Our search for deeper coherence is guided by a potentiality. We feel the slope toward deeper insight as we feel the direction in which a heavy weight is pulled along a steep incline. It is this dynamic intuition which guides the pursuit of discovery.[27]

Mystics view such experiences of direct, intuitive knowing as a foretaste of the development of intuitive consciousness, made possible by means of their science.

THE "INDIVISIBLE WHOLE"

Our ordinary way of knowing is through observation and analysis, apart from what is being known. Knowing is a process of comparing, remembering, reorganizing, and putting the known into relation with something else. For example, I know the earth circles the sun and I know my car holds twelve gallons of gas. I know the flight pattern of a marsh hawk. In my practice, I know when a patient is sad and about to cry: the lips quiver and the eyes get wet. I "know" all these things. But a different experience of knowing is also possible. For example, in a therapy group working with one of its members, I suddenly "know" the specific origin of the patient's conflict; I perceive the particulars clearly and my subsequent explorations with the patient yield "miraculous" success. Such perceptions are always correct, in contrast to those I gain when I apply a formula, raise questions in my mind, and proceed toward the probable — in short, when I make educated guesses. The quality of the intuitive experience is unique, and different from that of applying clinical wisdom or making predictions based on past history. My experience and reason must play a part, for intuitive understanding is not naive — it would not occur to someone unfamiliar with my field. But *how* do I know in this way?

A unified world is a prerequisite for intuition. To clarify, mystics describe their knowledge as knowledge by identity: the knower becomes one with the known rather than observing it. Such knowledge requires a metaphysic in which each person is connected in some way with everything else; it implies a field theory in which no absolute barriers exist between entities, but all entities respond and are unified within the field. In such a version of reality, consciousness, at some level, is coextensive with it. If we can partake of a consciousness that is not bounded by the physical brain but extends throughout existence, then subject and object are one, and we can know by being the object. In the West, such a statement is usually considered nonsensical, for it cannot be comprehended by reference to the object world, the world of discrete boundaries. The mystical view assumes a different organization of reality, one composed of gradients rather than boundaries. It posits a continuous flux in which entities exist, but not discretely, just as waves have individual existence but are continuous with each other, and with the ocean that gives rise to them and in which they merge. It goes a step further and considers every wave to be, simultaneously, every other wave, inseparable in time as well as space.

What makes such a world preposterous to us is our fixed perspective, based on the fundamental assumption of Western culture, an assumption that Alfred North Whitehead referred to as "simple location":

> When you are criticizing the philosophy of an epoch, do not chiefly direct your attention to those intellectual positions which its exponents feel it necessary explicitly to defend. There will be some fundamental assumptions which adherents of all the variant systems within the epoch unconsciously presupposed. Such assumptions appear so obvious that people do not know what they are assuming because no other way of putting things has ever occurred to them. With these assumptions, a certain limited number of types of philosophic systems are possible, and this group of systems constitutes the philosophy of the epoch.
>
> One such assumption underlies the whole philosophy of nature during the modern period. It is embodied in the conception which is supposed to express the most concrete aspect of nature. The Ionian philosophers asked "What is nature made of?" The answer is couched in terms of stuff, or matter, or material—the particular name chosen is indifferent—which has the property of simple location in space and time, or, if you adopt the more modern ideas, in space-time . . .
>
> The characteristic common both to space and time is that material can be said to be here in space and here in time, or here in space-time, in a perfectly definite sense which does not require for its explanation any reference to other regions of space-time.[28]

Whitehead wrote from the perspective provided in 1905 by Einstein's theory of special relativity. By 1932, Max Planck could declare:

In modern mechanics . . . it is impossible to obtain an adequate version of the laws for which we are looking, unless the physical system is regarded *as a whole*. According to modern mechanics (field theory), each individual particle of the system, in a certain sense, at any one time, exists simultaneously in every part of the space occupied by the system. This simultaneous existence applies not merely to the field of force with which it is surrounded, but also its mass and its charge.[29]

Consider de Broglie's 1958 statement:

In space-time everything which for each of us constitutes the past, the present and the future is given in block, and the entire collection of events, successive for each one of us, which form the existence of a material particle is represented by a line, the world line of the particle . . . each observer, as his time passes, discovers, so to speak, new slices of space-time which appear to him as successive aspects of the material world, though in reality the ensemble of events constituting space-time exist prior to his knowledge of them.[30]

Heisenberg explained how the theories of relativity and quantum mechanics led to concepts of time, space, and causality strikingly different from those we employ in the ordinary world through reason and the senses.[31] These concepts are so foreign that even physicists cannot "understand" them, cannot picture their workings. Nevertheless, scientists are forced to recognize the reality implied by these concepts by the data they produce in experiments in particle physics and astronomy. The world that emerges from such explorations can be described and employed only through the mathematics of four-dimensional "space/time," a mathematics based on the subatomic and galactic worlds.

The effect of such work is to prove empirically the illusory nature of the object world and the view of reality gained through the object self. Scientists conclude not that the reality of super-small and super-large is a special case, but rather that the reality of the ordinary object world is the special case, a limited interpretation that works only within the narrow zone of ordinary sensory data. Our customary view of the world and the logic we derive from it is a convenient illusion that shatters when we step outside its dimensions.

Our senses cannot perceive the new world that physicists have discovered through mathematics and suprasensory technology, which can transcend the boundaries of sensation and object-based logic. By employing special technology to extend ordinary perception, for example, cloud chambers, radio telescopes, and mass spectrographs, physicists have found a universe strikingly similar to that described by mystics — insofar as it can be described — a universe in which mystical intuition is possible. The discoveries of modern physics support the mystics' claim that the commonsense view — the world being composed of objects — is an illusion, because we tend to divide the world of experience into fixed entities, which we then order into fixed categories of time and space. The world is really a stream of activity in which forms appear and disappear, transient patterns in a dynamic, living flux whose basic formlessness mystics call a void or the Absolute.

Skeptics who find it difficult to acknowledge the reality of the Absolute need not shift their view too radically to perceive chinks in the coherence of the object world. Physicists, psychologists, and biologists agree that boundaries, which define the world, are more apparent than real.

Gardner Murphy has pointed out that our concept of biological boundaries is a function of the particular time and size scale we employ. Apparent boundaries are sensory phenomena that result from those scales; they are not absolutes. For example, we are constantly exchanging materials with the surrounding environment through respiration, eating, and elimination, a fact confirmed by radioisotope studies, which show that our bodies are constantly turning over materials and that we are not the same collection of atoms that we were a year ago. Bertalanffy summarized,

> As a result of its metabolism, which is characteristic of every living organism, its components are not the same from one moment to the next. Living forms are not in being, they are happening.[32]

Thus, bones and muscles are reinterpreted: what we call structures are actually slow processes of long duration, while what we call functions are quick processes of short duration. Thus, if we say that a function, such as a contraction of a muscle, is performed by a structure, it means that a quick and short process wave is superimposed on a long-lasting and slowly running wave. Activity, change, process — these are the "substances" of our bodies, of our world, and of the universe. Gradients, not boundaries, determine form.[33]

Mystics go further, claiming that the world of isolated objects perceived by our senses is not composed of a linear sequence of events, but rather is an interrelated, organic pattern of parallel and simultaneous relationships, of which linear relationships form a minor part. Physicists have arrived at a similar view:

> Quantum theory forces us to see the universe not as a collection of physical objects, but rather as a complicated web of relations between the various parts of a unified whole.[34]

Even the idea of "parts" — that is, separate entities — has been thrown into question by the implication of Bell's Theorem, a mathematical proof first published in 1964 and discussed more recently by the physicist d'Espignat.[35] In brief, Bell's Theorem states that if the statistical predictions of quantum mechanics are correct, "local realistic" theories are false in at least one of the three premises on which they are based: (1) realism (that "the world outside the self is

real and has at least some properties that exist independently
of human consciousness"); (2) inductive reasoning (that general conclusions can be reached by reasoning from particulars);
and (3) Einstein separability (that one particle cannot affect
another if it would have to propagate faster than the speed
of light).

Five out of seven experiments performed thus far support Bell's Theorem[36] and, according to d'Espignat, most
physicists have accepted it as being confirmed. Writes
d'Espignat, of the three premises listed above, Einstein separability is believed to be the most questionable.

> The doctrine that the world is made up of objects whose
> existence is independent of human consciousness turns out
> to be in conflict with quantum mechanics and with facts
> established by experiment.
> The violation of separability seems to imply that in some
> sense all these objects constitute an indivisible whole.

The full implications of Bell's Theorem are uncertain but
basically they constitute a profound revolution in the way we
view the world.

Thus, the revolution in physics may well confirm that
the universe is an "indivisible whole," which is necessary to
intuition's — direct knowing — taking place. Bell's Theorem
has led to d'Espignat's conclusion that the puzzle about how
knowledge of the world is possible at all appears to have a
natural solution that is compatible with knowledge through
being:

> To the extent that our minds and empirical reality are com-
> plementary sides of one and the same reality, it does not
> appear as highly surprising that the general structures of
> this reality should, on the one hand, be reflected in the
> mathematics we build up and, on the other hand, manifest
> themselves in empirical reality.[37]

Drawing parallels between the mathematically derived conclusions of particle physicists and the poetic utterances of mystics has its drawbacks, and writers like Capra and Zukav have received their share of criticism. Thomsen, while expressing appreciation for their attempts "to relate modern physics to other important concerns of humanity . . . particularly to mysticism and religion," warns that ideas in physics are always changing; indeed, two of Capra's concepts — the S-matrix theory and the bootstrap hypothesis — are now considered passé. Ideas in religion change also, and neither field can afford to be bound too closely to the other. Even worse, warns Thomsen, a too-easy equation of one with the other could lead to quasi-scientific cults and gurus.[38] In fact, ultimate reality is beyond formulation.

Bernstein takes a similar view:

> The science of the present will look as antiquated to our successors as much of the nineteenth-century science looks to us now. To hitch a religious philosophy to a contemporary science is a sure route to obsolescence.[39]

Nevertheless, however appropriate the concerns of these critics may be, the fact is that modern physicists are engaged in mystical-sounding speculations to which they are forced by the facts of the physical world. If these same debates over the meaning of Bell's Theorem or even the implication of quantum mechanics were not dignified by the names of respected physicists, they would pejoratively be labeled "mystical." Although similarities in physicists' and mystics' interpretations of the world should not be taken as evidence that their versions are equivalent, the views of the former should lend some credence to those of the latter, at least justifying a more serious investigation of the mystical tradition.

The universe newly discovered by modern physics is characterized by unity, simultaneity, and human consciousness as an interacting dimension of that world. In identifying these features, Western science establishes a realistic basis for the operation of mystical intuition. In the face of these discoveries, one can hope that Western thinkers will come to accept the possibility of direct knowledge, thus finding themselves ready to accept mystical science as a straightforward, empirical process dealing with the development of a basic human capacity.

Part II
THE SELF

6

The Object Self

The basic difference between Western psychology and the mystical tradition lies in our assumptions about the self. We regard the self as a type of object, localized to the body and separate from other objects; mysticism considers that belief to be an illusion because it applies only to a limited aspect of human life. Mystics insist there is a Self, masked by ordinary consciousness, unbound by space and time, that can be both individual and universal — as with the wave that exists and then merges completely with the ocean from which it has never been separated and whose substance is its own.

Because it seems so obvious to us that each person is a finite biological entity, capable of communicating with others but essentially alone, the perspective of mystical science will not seem credible unless we first can appreciate that we have learned to think of ourselves in this way during childhood — that object self is not given, a priori. Furthermore, we do have indications that we can experience a different self.

In this chapter I quote passages from the fields of developmental psychology and psychotherapy, which are as "spiritual" as most texts found in esoteric bookstores because they deal with the psychological reality bearing on "Who am I?" "Why am I?" — uncontaminated by the terminology of archaic mystical systems.

65

THE WORLD AT BIRTH

We imagine that the newborn infant opens its eyes to the world as we see it now, except that our world may be unfocused and incomprehensible to a mind that has almost no prior experience. Yet we cannot be certain about our supposition because we know very little about the consciousness of infancy: we do not remember it and infants cannot tell us about it. Consequently, for centuries philosophers and psychologists could only speculate on the fascinating question of how the world appears to an infant who sees it for the first time. The careful, systematic observations of infant behavior of Piaget, Gesell, Spitz, Wolff, and others have gone far toward providing us with a basis for conjecture, but modern surgery has given us the most direct evidence of how our world first appears.

Specifically, Marius von Senden reported on sixty-three persons whose blindness since birth resulted from cataracts but whose sight had been surgically restored.[1] Removal of the cataracts permitted them to see for the first time. At the time of the operations these subjects were between three and forty-three years old, with most in their teens or twenties. Unlike newborn infants, these people could communicate the nature of their initial experience.

Von Senden's "twice-born" subjects, when they first saw the world, experienced an amorphous, confusing field of color and light without any meaning; indeed, they felt the visual stimuli to be intrusive and disturbing and required weeks of practice to learn to recognize simple objects. For example, after much effort one patient was able to recognize a pencil held vertically, but when the pencil was rotated 90 degrees, his recognition disappeared, and he had to relearn perception of the pencil. The difficulties were so great that some of the patients gave up the effort, retreating from the "gift" of sight and expressing the wish to return to the ordered world of sound, touch, and smell that had been so familiar and manageable before the surgery. Not only were they unable to use vision, but the influx of new stimuli interfered with the efficiency of the old system.

We cannot regard these findings as conclusive because there are important differences between the reactions of von Senden's patients and those of a newborn infant. For example, Peter Wolff discovered that infants do not shy away from novel stimuli but attend to them from the first day, with their attentiveness increasing as they grow older.[2] Unlike von Senden's patients, they give every indication of eager assimilation and curiosity about the visual world. Of course, for infants, visual stimuli are no more unfamiliar than those of hearing or touch. René Spitz noted,

> By contrast, the newborn has no world image at all, no stimuli from any sensory modality that he can recognize as signals; even by the time he is six months old, only very few such signals have been laid down and established as memory traces. Therefore, stimuli impinging on the infant's sensorium are as alien in the visual as in all the other sensory modalities.[3]

Spitz also noted that infants are protected from being overwhelmed by stimulation. There appears to be a "stimulus barrier" arising from the infants' neurological immaturity, the great amount of time they spend asleep, the selective filtering of stimuli, and the protection afforded by the special environment usually provided for them, especially by the physically protective mother.

Although these differences exist, the work of Wolff, Spitz, Piaget, and others gives us justification for believing that the infants' initial experience of the world is as amorphous as that of von Senden's patients. Research supports the idea that infants too must learn to perceive — to make sense of incoming stimuli and to assign them meaning — and that they do so through interaction with the environment, both human and inanimate. Infants and young children learn things that later, as adults, they assume they always knew. For example, they learn that the environment is composed of objects and that they and other people are objects, separate and distinct from each other. Thought and language develop during the same period and are structured by the same experiences. For example, in a typical scene a mother holds an object, a ball, so that the baby can see it and reach for it. "Ball," the mother says. "See the ball! Ball!" The baby reaches for it, eyes focused, breathing fast, making sounds, "Baw, baw." The baby grasps the ball and immediately places it in its mouth — its primary organ for testing and assimilating the world. They coordinate language, thought, vision, and muscle movement in the learning process and, consequently, word, image, and touch combine to form the concept ball.

As the work of Piaget and Erikson makes clear, we use our bodies as templates to understand the world. Consider one of Piaget's experiments: A child is presented with the problem of opening a box with a lid. How does he solve it? He turns it in his hands, struggling with the puzzle. Suddenly, he opens his mouth, then the box.[4] He uses his body as an object to understand the box, to contact and organize the world. Such experiences establish the structure of our thoughts, teaching the body rules that we have learned. Ultimately, our most abstract and fundamental concepts are built upon the equation: object = body = self. For example, our concepts of space, time, and causality are actually the space, time, and causality that pertain to the world of objects. Useful and necessary as these conceptual structures may be, they form a barrier to perceiving a reality whose dimensions exceed those of the object world. The barrier, because acquired so early and, in the absence of alternative experience, utterly convincing, is hard to transcend.

Awareness itself can provide that alternative experience because it does not have object properties and is an anomaly in the object world. However, the awareness of awareness develops late. At first, the physical is dominant. The observations of Louise Ames on the social behavior of eighteen-month-old children illustrates the dominance of the concrete in young children's experience of others and, by inference, of themselves:

> Eighteen-month-old children mostly treat contemporaries as physical objects or disregard them completely. Five in one room may disregard one of the others. If two were together near an object, one may just push the other out of the way impersonally, as though he were an object . . . one as [he] climbs, pushes a second, who falls on a third. All ignore this. Or two may try to climb up in exactly the same place. Both struggle with each other, but merely for the space, not aggressively as later. Child wanting to sit on chair filled by other child may either sit *on* child or may spill him out. May walk around or just bump into other child.[5]

We might infer that since the children do not perceive other children to be conscious, feeling beings, their own sense of subjective self is slight, if present at all. Arnold Gesell reports that in a twelve-month-old child, about to walk, "even the sense of personal possession is practically absent and he makes very meager distinction between himself and others."[6]

The behavior of infants aside from sleeping or eating indicates a primary drive to act on the environment, exploring, assimilating, controlling, and possessing whatever can be reached. Of necessity, there is a premium on the ability to perceive and manipulate objects, and perceptual and cognitive learning is devoted to that task. Interestingly, the urge to possess precedes the sense of a self that possesses. This is illustrated by the fact that possessive pronouns appear first. Gesell notes that at twenty-four months of age, "Pronouns *mine, me, you* and *I* are coming into use approximately in order just given."[7] "Mine" leads to "me" (the object) and "you" (the object) and only later does "I" (the subject) appear. However, when "I" emerges, it too is treated as an object.

Through the second year, the child's egocentricity and possessiveness increase:

> Relations with children are tentative . . . verbalization is largely directed toward obtaining or protecting objects. Child grabs what he wants but is more interested in object obtained than the person from whom it is obtained. Child cannot share. He is still consolidating a sense of self by obtaining and hoarding possessions. "Mine" is a favorite word.[8]

However, at about thirty-six months:

> [the child] . . . no longer seems to need to confirm and embellish self with possessions. There is less domineering, less violence and fewer threats of violence in his relations with other children . . . he begins to say "we." At three and a half years of age a sense of self that extends to other children is in evidence. At this age the child is beginning to establish himself with his contemporaries, aligning with some and excluding others. He now treats other children as individual persons with special individual characteristics.

Thus, at three years of age children begin to recognize and be interested in other children as feeling beings like themselves. Pure possession yields to social interests, and the child's world expands greatly. Nevertheless, the first three years establish a basic mode of consciousness, an integrated way of perceiving the world that operates automatically and has as its cornerstone the object self. The "object mode" is functional, adapted to the need to act on the environment. It emphasizes the perception of differences and boundaries, the structuring of diffuse stimuli into manipulable entities. Its utility is easy to understand. For example, in trying to obtain food by hunting (or driving a taxicab), one needs sharply focused vision; consciousness must include a clear sense of past, present, and future; planning, remembering, and calculating must take place. The self in such a mode of consciousness is an object, just as a deer or automobiles are objects; the self of ordinary experience, finite and distinct from other entities, makes up that world. In this way, the object mode enables the organism to act on the environment and thus to survive. Self-preservation and acquisition are the primary motives of the object self, and these motives both serve the object self and reinforce it. Thus, the way we perceive the world, our mode of consciousness, is a function of our purpose. The type of self we experience is integral to that mode, calling it forth and being sustained by it.

Initially, the object self is necessary for psychological as well as physical survival. Indeed, failure to establish a sense of one's own boundaries leads to retarded development and psychosis. However, the object self, once created, does not give up control and finally dominates consciousness. The tyranny of the object self has unfortunate consequences, for we are more than objects and have needs the object mode cannot fulfill.

In contrast, the intention to receive from the environment (as in listening to music), rather than to act on it, as the hunter must, requires a different mode of consciousness, one that diminishes the sense of boundaries and permits the experience of merging with the environment. This "receptive mode" is associated with a different sense of self than the hunter's or taxi driver's, one less discrete, less prominent; past and future drop away and sensual attributes dominate over the perception of form and verbal meaning. Analytic thought tends to cease; attention becomes diffuse and boundaries blur. The separate self dissolves, permitting the experience of connection or merging into the environment. Awareness of awareness becomes possible.

The following table summarizes the characteristics of the two modes.

COMPARISON OF MODES

	Object Mode	Receptive Mode
Purpose:	To act on the environment	To receive the environment
Self:	Objectlike, localized, separate from others	Undifferentiated, nonlocalized, not distinct from environment, blurring or merging of boundaries
	Vantage point from which world is seen	
	Self-centered awareness	World-centered awareness
World:	Objects	Process
	Absolute time	Relative time
	Linear causality	Simultaneity
Consciousness:	Focal attention	Diffuse attention
	Sharp perceptual and cognitive boundaries	Blurred boundaries
	Logical thought, reasoning	Paralogic, intuition, fantasy
	Formal dominates sensual	Sensual dominates formal
	Past/Future	Now
Communication:	Language	Music/art/poetry
Neurophysiology:	Sympathetic nervous system	Parasympathetic system
	Left hemisphere dominates	Right hemisphere dominates
	EEG: increased beta waves decreased alpha and theta waves	EEG: decreased beta waves increased alpha and theta waves

To some extent, the different functions of the two modes parallel those of the left and right brain hemispheres. The linear organization characteristic of the left side of the brain corresponds to the characteristics of the object mode, while the right side deals more with patterned holistic perception and shows considerable correspondence with the receptive mode.

At birth, the receptive mode is dominant, but as we mature it is progressively superseded because survival requires manipulation of the objects needed for survival. The receptive mode does not substitute for the object mode; indeed, the functions of one mode cannot be performed in the other. The taxi driver struggling to get a passenger to the airport and contending with heavy traffic had better be in the object mode: in precise control of the automobile, with sharp boundary perceptions, optimum muscle tension, and good object logic. However, if lovers treat each other like objects, attempting to control their partners and maintaining a clear and separate sense of self, they are likely to experience "screwing" rather than "making love."

Both modes are necessary. We know that creative problem solving involves two phases, corresponding to these two modes. The first phase requires the object mode, with its active, vigorous, controlled thinking: assembling data, examining logical relationships, striving toward a resolution of the difficulty. Typically, one reaches an impasse. Then, one relaxes and shifts attention to something else, leading to the second phase. Suddenly, in a state of relaxation or "drifting" thought (the receptive mode), the solution appears. Such "inspirations" occur just prior to falling asleep or waking; sometimes they occur while one is listening to music or in reverie. The receptive mode permits a synthesis, a merging of what the object mode had kept separate.

Control is primary to the object mode, while the receptive mode requires "letting go," "allowing," rather than making it happen. The importance of control enabled by the object mode was conveyed to me vividly during my internship when I assisted at a neurosurgical operation at 3:00 A.M. Because of my fatigue and the early morning hour, the objectivity and detachment with which I had been functioning began to weaken. As the smell of the cauterizing scalpel struck my nostrils, I began to perceive the exposed brain before me as the brain of a person like myself, and the *emotional meaning* of the cuts being made in the fragile brain tissue suddenly evoked an intense, visceral response. I became giddy, almost fainted, and had to withdraw from the operating table. Prior to that incident, I had assisted at a number of operations that could have evoked an equally strong reaction, were it not for the object mode of consciousness with which I had learned to perform. On this occasion the object mode broke down and the receptive mode reorganized the dimensions of my experience. The result was dysfunction for that particular task.

One may experience the opposite example — the importance of changing from the object mode to the receptive — in visiting a museum. People usually enter museums in the object mode of consciousness and stroll quickly past the paintings and statues, giving only five to ten seconds of attention to each. (The next time you are in a museum check this for yourself.) The museum's impact on the visitor in that mode produces tired feet and a "stuffed" sensation in the head. The experience is disappointing because one can only receive what art can give when one is in the receptive mode. The mode of consciousness with which a person drives an automobile or performs most work is not appropriate to communing with a work of art. If the museumgoer were to settle down in front of one particular painting, relinquish active thinking, and simply allow the painting to express itself to him or her, the experience would become something quite different — a source of satisfaction, psychological nourishment, and refreshment. The "presence" of the painting would go out to the viewer, rather than the viewer attacking the painting with his or her stare. This difference is reflected in a poem by Rainer Maria Rilke, "The Archaic Torso of Apollo":

> We did not know his legendary head,
> in which the eyeball ripened. But
> his torso still glows like a candelabrum
> in which his gaze, only turned low,
> holds and gleams. Else could not the curve
> of the breast blind you, nor in the slight turn
> of the loins could a smile be running
> to the middle, which carried procreation.

Else would this stone be standing maimed and short
below the shoulders' translucent plunge nor flimmering
like the fell of beasts of prey
nor breaking out of all its contours like a star; for
there is no place that does not see you. You must
change your life.[10]

This work of art is not an inert object but a vital force that can affect the viewer, if allowed to by the appropriate mode of consciousness.

It should be noted that the receptive mode is not "higher consciousness," not the goal of mysticism. For mystical science, the receptive mode, in harmony with the object mode, provides the necessary base from which further development ensues. The less-defined self, the attitude of allowing, the sensitivity to a wide range of perceptual cues are important capacities for students in mystical schools.

From the point of view of psychotherapy, a person's ability to adopt the receptive mode is of considerable importance in, among other things, increasing his or her satisfaction and enhancing empathic communication. For this reason, understanding the interrelationship of motivation, mode of consciousness, and self-experience can be useful in achieving psychotherapeutic goals.

The functions that the receptive mode provides are necessary to complement the object mode as it increasingly dominates perception and excludes from awareness dimensions not emphasized in that mode. For example, the object mode is characterized by an emphasis on formal characteristics of objects, rather than on the sensual. To illustrate, Shapiro reported on research in which children of different age groups were given a Rorschach test.[11] In their responses to the ink blots, a definite trend was apparent: the youngest groups responded primarily to the color and texture of the pictures, but the older groups paid progressively more attention to the shape and meaning. It is reasonable to assume that our actual experience of the world changes as we grow older because we attend to different aspects of it; different dimensions of reality occupy our attention.

Similarly, we come to perceive ourselves exclusively as objects, while we seldom experience the subjective self, the "I" of awareness — so different from any object. When we do, we regard it as unreal or assign it to the domain of objects.

Certain mystical techniques can be understood, in part, as bringing about a shift toward a greater balance of the two modes, usually involving an increase in the receptive. The effect of such a shift is to open the student to dimensions of reality obscured by the object mode.

7

Motivation, Virtue, and Consciousness

We have seen how motivation shapes consciousness. The object mode, in its focus on control and acquisition, is at variance with the perception of an interconnected, unified reality. To the extent that you are selfish you cannot experience an identity any larger than the object self. The virtues traditionally practiced in mysticism and religion can be understood to establish a motivational base different from that of the object mode, thus permitting a form of perception and cognition that can perceive and appreciate the connections, rather than the separation, between people and things.

Religions, while the prescribe the virtuous life, have a strong tendency to emphasize reward and punishment. People therefore tend to practice virtues within religions the way some schoolchildren perform for a teacher — to earn a good grade or the gratification of the teacher's attention and praise. Examined closely, such "virtuous" activity begins to resemble a commercial enterprise: the accumulation of heavenly credit, duly noted by a divine accountant, in a layaway plan for life after death. Such is not the role of virtue in mystical science. "I will not serve God like a laborer, in expectation of my wages," said Rabia, the Sufi saint.[1]

Western observers are often confused by the mystic's approach to virtue. Indeed, they frequently associate piety with mysticism, since the practice of virtues has indeed been an important part of mystical science — more important, in fact, than many of the techniques that seem more interesting. In the Upanishads, for example, the primary instruction is to "purify the heart" in order to see Brahman, to become "free from desires" in order to know Truth:

> When all the desires that dwell in the heart fall away, then the mortal becomes immortal and here attains Brahman.
> When all the ties of the heart are severed here on earth, then the mortal becomes immortal. This much alone is the teaching.[2]

Buddha was more explicit and prescribed charity, kindness, humility, patience, and calm for his disciples. Similar qualities are said to be necessary for students of Sufism.

But piety, for its own sake is not the point. In mystical science, virtuous behavior is prescribed as a necessary step in the development of intuitive perception. Mystics understand the relationship between motivation, mode of consciousness, and perception. They know that virtuous behavior leads to specific psychological effects essential to their goal.

In this light, a mystic's motive for behaving virtuously differs sharply from that of a religious devotee, and this distinction shows mysticism to be a psychological science rather than a belief system. The desire for heaven or fear of hell — chief motivations for virtuous living within religions — are said to be inimical to the development of intuitive perception. According to the mystical texts, a teacher can bestow nothing. The teacher of mysticism can only help to equip a suitable student for receiving Knowledge — that is, enlightenment. Knowledge cannot be withheld from a student who is ready for it; neither can it be given to a student who is unqualified to receive it. The ability to receive Knowledge is a functional matter, having nothing to do with reward or punishment in the usual sense. Thus, one does not "earn" enlightenment, one becomes capable of receiving it.

THE FUNCTION OF RENUNCIATION

But why, since reward is not involved, does mysticism require that the "heart be purified"? Why is it necessary for the student to be "free from desire," even the desire for heaven, or enlightenment? In short, how does virtuous behavior contribute to mystical development? For simplicity, let us consider a single activity, "renunciation," which is held to be virtuous and necessary both to the traditional practice of the mystics and to the outward forms of religious institutions. Renunciation is usually thought of as ascetic behavior: chastity or poverty or living in a cave or adopting a vegetarian diet. Actually, renunciation is an *attitude*. Renunciation means giving up one's attachment to the things of the world, an attachment based on the wish to possess them.

A Zen master remarked, "Renunciation is not giving up the things of this world, it is accepting that they go away."[3] The result of such acceptance is fulfillment, not deprivation. Renunciation does not mean giving up any activity per se and withdrawing from the everyday world. In the Bhagavad Gita even warfare can be pursued in the spirit of renunciation. The Vedic literature is clear on this point. "It is not action, but the desire for the result that brings suffering. Therefore, the doer is asked to relinquish all attachment to the result."[4]

Mysticism is concerned with going beyond the object self. If we recall that a principal function of that self is to possess, we can see that renunciation makes possible a type of consciousness that is different from the object mode. When the latter is operating, no matter what a person strives for – money, virtue, or heaven – the basic intention is the same: to possess; and possession reinforces the object self. Indeed, it is only the object self – defined by its separateness from other things – that can possess.

The desire to possess is called "greed," and in mystical science the term is descriptive rather than judgmental. The problem is not that greed is "bad"—in early development it is necessary for survival—but that greed has psychological consequences. Specifically, the intention to possess not only intensifies the object self, but it engenders fear of the loss of that which is possessed. The ultimate fear is of death, because death results in the loss of all possessions *and* the object self.

It is hard to find a neurotic symptom or a human vice that cannot be traced to the desire to possess or the fear of loss. For this reason, as well, it is not surprising that renunciation—that is, relinquishing possessiveness—is emphasized in the mystical tradition. In the Buddhist texts, in fact, renunciation is prescribed as a cure for all human suffering. We can understand that neurotic symptoms might disappear as a byproduct of a process that diminishes the dominance of the object self.

Ultimately, renunciation, selflessness, and virtuous behavior, in general, are necessary because they reflect the nature of reality, the way things are:

HIS OWN SUFFERING

Whenever the rabbi of Sasov saw anyone's suffering, either of spirit or of body, he shared it so earnestly that the other's suffering became his own. Once someone expressed his astonishment at this capacity to share in another's troubles. "What do you mean 'share'?" said the rabbi. "It is my own sorrow; how can I help but suffer it?"[5]

Arriving at such understanding is not easy, partly because we do not perceive the extent to which our customary view, based on the object self, is a distortion. As a result, most of our behavior is self-centered, regardless of outward appearances.

We seldom notice the subtle hypocrisies indigenous to our own culture, the accepted rationalizations whereby we ignore the needs of others, or the vanity fed by overt acts of "generosity," or the pride maintained by righteousness, whether moral or intellectual. Mystical science pays the great-est attention to these areas because you can't fool your own consciousness; it takes the form suited to your real intentions.

In contrast to mysticism, Western psychotherapy focuses on the idiosyncratic distortions stemming from one's personal history and tends to neglect the cultural distortion, the sanctioned self-deceit in which therapists participate. It would be of considerable value to psychotherapists if they became more aware of the way in which they and their pa-tients seek gratification and reinforcement of the object self, thereby becoming vulnerable to anxiety and reinforcing the possessive behavior of others. This point is made in another story from the Hasidic tradition:

THE RABBI OF LUBLIN AND A PREACHER

A famous traveling maggid was once preaching in a city, when word came that the rabbi of Lublin had arrived. And immediately all the maggid's audience left to greet the zad-dik. The preacher found himself quite alone. He waited for a little while and then he too saw the Seer's table heaped with the "ransom-money" which petitioners and other visi-tors had brought him. The maggid asked: "How is this pos-sible! I have been preaching here for days and have gotten nothing, while all this came your way in a single hour!"

Rabbi Yitzhak replied: "It is probably because each wakens in the hearts of men what he cherishes in his own heart: I, the hatred of money, and you the love of it."[6]

By heightening sensitivity to these matters, the mystical tradition can help us acquire a more sophisticated awareness of self-centered behavior.

THE FUNCTION OF HUMILITY

Other virtues can also be viewed as significant purely in terms of function. Consider humility and sincerity, both of which are required of students of mystical science. These vir-tues are necessary for learning. Humility is the acceptance of the possibility that someone else can teach you something you do not already know, especially about yourself. Conversely, pride and arrogance close the doors of the mind. Thus, in the process of mystical development, for which a teacher is necessary, humility is a functional necessity.

THE FUNCTION OF SINCERITY

Mystics define sincerity as honesty of intention. People may think they desire to learn when what they actually want is to receive attention. When the attention is taken away, they lose interest and leave to seek other sources of "learning." It can be observed in any educational system that if the dominant wish of a student is to be fed with praise or attention, the learning that takes place will be very limited, regardless of what the student may think is taking place. This is especially true if the learning requires self-initiated effort. After all, physiological and psychological survival require that we be efficient at obtaining what we *actually* want, not what we *say* we want, or even what we *think* we want.

Sincerity is said to be the primary requirement for the student of mystical science. Again, the practice of this virtue is not a moral matter but a functional one — we find what we seek. The biological analogy of this principle can be discerned in infants during the first month of life. Rubinow and Frankel demonstrated that the newborn infant recognizes food only when he is hungry. Spitz comments further:

Actually he does not recognize milk as such, nor the bottle, nor the rubber nipple, nor the breast, nor anything else. He "recognizes," if one can say so, the nipple when he receives it in the mouth, and in response to this stimulus he usually begins to suck. However, even this elementary form of perception has to be qualified. If the infant happens to be concerned with something else, if, for instance, he is screaming because his need for food has not been immediately satisfied, he will not react to the nipple, even when it is inserted into his mouth, but will go on screaming. It will take prolonged oral stimulation to make him direct his attention again to the food for which he is screaming, and which had been available to him all the time.[7]

We may paraphrase this situation as follows: if seekers of mystical knowledge are sincere (actually "hungering" for Truth, rather than for praise, security, attention, and so on), they will be able to respond to the special "nutrition" the teaching provides. However, if the student's consciousness is dominated by vanity, possessiveness, impatience, or fear, these states will block the necessary perception and render the student incapable of receiving what is offered. Such students are described as being too "raw" and are sent away, not as punishment, but because their attitude renders them unable to gain anything from a teacher or a school. The beginning student is not expected to be completely free from interfering desires or from egocentricity, but these factors must be sufficiently controlled so that they do not prevent the teaching process from operating. For this reason people approaching mystical science must first go through a preparatory stage of "learning how to learn." During this stage they may not encounter any of the activities for which they are eager or have come to expect, such as meditation, sacrifice, austerity, and the like. All of these would be distorted and diverted from their potential usefulness by the student's importunate state, as with the infant who cannot recognize a nipple when the infant is completely wrapped up in screaming for food.

The problem is not unknown in psychotherapy. Patients seek therapy because they want their suffering to be relieved, but they have their own ideas of how that can be accomplished. Usually their theory is that the therapist will give them what they believe they lack: love, security, confidence, satisfaction, and so forth. The therapist, who knows that what the patient wants will not solve the problem, must use that initial motivation, incorrect as it may be, to enable patients to realize the true nature of their problem: namely, that it is they themselves who interfere with receiving what they want. They must come to see the falseness of their assumptions about themselves and the world. To paraphrase the dilemma experienced by one such patient: "Others may think that I am all right, but if they knew what I was really like they would hate me. Therefore, my best strategy is to hide my real feelings and thoughts. Why are people so boring?"

To correct those assumptions, lessons learned early in development from parents and society must be seen for what they are, not accepted as final truth. But if a patient insists too strongly on gratifying his or her wishes in therapy, the necessary clarification will not take place; an impasse will be reached in which no further progress is possible. However, if a person can tolerate the necessary frustration, he or she can begin to benefit from what a therapist can actually provide: assistance in perceiving reality.

The importance of motivation is illustrated in numerous teaching stories, as well as in the occurrences of everyday life. Spitz gives an account of an experiment by Wolfgang Kohler that could be used as a teaching story without altering a word:

> A dog was offered a piece of meat from which he was separated by a long high wire fence, open at both ends. Under normal circumstances the dog was able to solve the problem without any difficulty, by circling the fence and grabbing the meat. However, when the dog was starved for several days, he could not tear himself away from the close proximity of the meat to circle the fence but went rushing to get close to the meat — a conflict ending in exhaustion after desperate and futile attempts to climb the fence.[8]

Too much hunger — or too little — and the student will not progress.

However, a qualification concerning virtuous behavior is in order. Renunciation, humility, and sincerity can have different meanings to the mystic and to the average person, especially when the inner attitude rather than external appearance is held to be crucial. For example, one mystic defined generosity as "doing justice without requiring justice."[9] Only when such understanding is reached can virtue be said to be a manifestation of what is real, independent of custom and time. Thus, chastity, meaning abstention from sexual intercourse, is only an outward behavior. In mystical science, the virtue of chastity resides in an attitude and is not necessarily dependent on sexual activity or its absence.

The Rabbi of Sasov experienced another man's suffering as his own. This unity of all human beings, their interconnection and interdependence, is the primary vision of mysticism. It says that the virtue mystics practice is necessary not only because of its functional utility but because it is realistic. One should treat the other as oneself because below the surface we are all aspects of one being; the Golden Rule is not an arbitrary, culturally determined morality but an expression of the actual nature of the world. Our continued existence as a species and our further development depend on our capacity for recognizing this reality despite the compelling influence of the object self. As in intuition, the discoveries of modern physics provide considerable support for postulating the connectedness of all being. The viewpoint of mysticism finds further support in the field of psychology, where the research of Kohlberg suggests that morality develops in progressive and irreversible stages whose direction points to the reality that mystical science affirms, rather than the world view of scientific empiricism.

MORAL DEVELOPMENT

The virtues are means to an end, an end reached by a developmental process: "Buddhas and Boddhisatvas are not enlightened by fixed teachings but by an intuitive process that is spontaneous and natural."[10] There is evidence that the virtues themselves are the product of a developmental process, perhaps the same one that moves to enlightenment. According to psychoanalytic theory, morality is a function of superego development, of introjection of parental standards during childhood. However, Kohlberg's studies contradict that assumption and suggest that moral judgment is a result of the development of broad social-cognitive capacities and values rather than of a "superego" or "introjections of parental standards":

> The development of moral judgment cannot be explained by a nondevelopmental view of moral learning as simply the internalization of cultural rules through verbal learning, reinforcement, or identification . . . the data suggests that the natural aspects of moral development are continuous and a reaction to the whole social world rather than a product of a certain stage, a certain concept (reciprocity), or certain types of social relations (peer relations).[11]

In his pioneering studies, Piaget described the first stage of morality, found in children from four to eight years of age, as "moral realism." He attributed it to two defects of judgment: (1) egocentrism — the confusion of one's own perspective with that of others, resulting in an inability to see moral values as relative to different people or goals, and (2) realism — the confusion of subjective phenomena with objective things, resulting in the belief that moral rules are fixed and external rather than a product of particular cultural expectations. A person at the moral realism stage judges an act by assessing its conformity to a rule rather than by evaluating its motive and regards rules as unchangeable, regardless of circumstances. Such an individual recognizes one perspective only. He or she defines wrong by the fact that an act is punished and focuses on severe, painful punishment of the wrongdoer rather than restitution to the victim. In addition, such a person believes that violation of the rules will lead the natural world to injure the culprit.

Kohlberg found that these aspects of primitive moral judgment change regularly through adolescence and adulthood. In reviewing the research done in this area, he concluded:

> . . . moral internalization relates closely to the cognitive development of moral concepts [this finding] contrasts mark-

edly with prevailing theories in the area. Learning theorists interested in overt behavior, psychoanalysts interested in fantasy, and Piaget, interested in moral judgment, have all assumed that the basic features of adult conscience have developed by early childhood (ages five to eight). This assumption as to the age of appearance of conscience is required if morality is to be derived from an intense unilateral relationship of identification with the parent. It is also required if . . . conscience or the sense of obligation are to be seen as survivals of infantile experience rather than as reactions to more adult experience of the world. Actually, moral judgment data suggests that anything clearly like "conscience" develops quite late.[12]

Kohlberg conducted a twenty-year longitudinal study of the development of moral judgment in American males and concluded that moral judgment developed through six qualitatively different stages and formed an unvarying sequence. Testing his subjects at three-year intervals, he found that they had either stayed at the same stage or had progressed one stage further. None regressed, as measured by his test. The stages could be legitimately considered to be specific cognitive structures because the subjects reasoned at the same stage, or, at most, one stage higher or lower, regardless of the particular problem they were given to judge.

Each higher moral stage is logically more advanced, . . . as defined in Piaget's work. Moral judgment, however, is not simply logical reasoning applied to moral problems. In the first place, moral judgment involves role-taking, taking the point of view of others . . . we have argued at length elsewhere that rational moral judgments must be universalizable, consistent, and reversible. Each higher moral stage meets these formal conditions better than its predecessor.[13]

Subjects in stage six formed moral judgments by the following three-step process: (1) taking the role of each person in the situation and considering the claims he might make; (2) imagining they did not know which person in the situation they would be and asking themselves which claims they would give up; and (3) basing their judgments on those "fully" reversible" claims — that is, those they would choose to uphold, not knowing who in the situation they were to be. Such "reversible" thinking is the real basis for the Golden Rule.

Kohlberg's data, then, contradict the notion that morality is learned primarily from parents or peers. The fact that subjects in stage six invariably used reversible thinking in making moral judgments supports the idea that ethics are not arbitrary, cultural artifacts but have a universal, absolute basis. The six-stage process of development seems to indicate that that basis — truly virtuous — is approached through a developmental process that marks the psychological maturity of human beings. This growth process can be seen as corresponding with the mystical concept of the evolution of consciousness: becoming able to perceive the oneness of all being.

Thus, in many traditions we find the story of a person who knocks on God's door seeking admission:

"Who is there?" God asks.
"It is I."
"Go away!" God replies.

Sometime later, the person returns and knocks again:

"Who is there?" God asks.
"It is Thou."
"Enter," God replies.

Kohlberg's findings empirically confirm this developmental direction, which has not been acknowledged by Western psychology but is fundamentally significant. His findings give credence to the mystics' claim that they are interested in furthering the development of the natural capacity and destiny of human beings.

By understanding the functional importance of traditional virtues — their realistic basis — psychotherapists can modify the amoral "scientific" stance they tend to bring to the therapeutic setting. It is one thing to be nonjudgmental in order to establish a safe situation in which patients can more easily explore their thoughts and feelings; it is another to rest the nonjudgmental stance on the belief that morality is only arbitrary, having no substantive basis in a random universe. Actually, few therapists succeed in behaving with such prescribed neutrality. The goal of therapy is often conceptualized as the maximizing of the patient's freedom of choice, but it is assumed that the free choice will prove to be ethical. If the choice were to murder, for example, that choice would be assumed to be pathological.

By understanding the relationship of motivation to mode of consciousness and the type of self we experience, we have the means for differentiating and assessing motives on a basis other than social compatibility or productivity. In the case of greed versus generosity, for example, it can be clear that possessiveness leads to fear of loss, to insatiability, and to the experience of a contained, guarded, isolated self. In contrast, real generosity results in freedom, diminished anxiety, and a self connected to others.

The issue is far larger than that of improving psychotherapy. At stake are the quality, the significance, and the future of human life. Moral relativism has deprived us of the support for traditional virtues that had been provided by a theological perspective. Without that support it will be hard to find our way in the dark landscape that has followed Hiroshima. Yet there is an alternative to moral chaos that does not require a return to the Middle Ages: the realization that "no man is an island" refers to the actual nature of reality. Traditional virtues are consistent with the underlying reality and provide the possibility of *knowing* that reality. Virtues prepare the mind for a more advanced perception.

8

The Observing Self

Although it is helpful to understand that meaning and direction exist and that a larger self and world can eventually be perceived, intellectual understanding is no substitute for the actual experience of that reality. It is the task of mystical science to bring people to that experience. To do so, it first employs a number of techniques whose function is to enhance what I will call *the observing self*. Modern Western psychotherapy performs a similar function of enhancement, although it does not recognize it, and it is possible to understand the operation of seemingly diverse schools of therapy on the basis of that activity. However, psychotherapy relies on the theoretical structure of Western psychology and psychoanalysis, which is defective because its center is missing: it does not recognize the observing self as the center of all experience, assigning it to a peripheral position. This error results in much confusion and impedes progress in the field. The mystical tradition can make a major contribution to Western culture by bringing to its attention this observing center of human experience with all its implications for the nature of human beings and the universe in which they exist.

Before discussing the observing self it is necessary to clarify the phenomenological basis of the word *self*, because

91

most schools of psychotherapy concern themselves with a particular realm of self-experience. Indeed, we can gain considerable clarity in reading the psychiatric literature by noticing which realm is emphasized by a particular school. Basically, the phenomenon to which the word *self* applies derives from four domains of experience: (1) thought, (2) feeling, (3) functional capacity, and (4) the observing center. Experiencing these domains convinces us of our locality in space and of our unique psychological identity. Memory, which applies to all four domains, convinces us of our continuity in time.

THE THINKING SELF

For most of us, the self with which we are most concerned is that of the first domain — thinking. Planning, solving problems, worrying, imagining — this self seems to be in charge, controlling our immediate activities and the course of our lives. We consider it responsible for what we do and do not do.

This domain contains the conceptual self, that is, the idea of who and what one is. The conceptual self has dual aspects. One is the "me" defined by others — parents, friends, teachers, colleagues, and the culture generally — who say: "You are dumb, (pretty, ugly, shy, strong, weak)" — and on and on. "You are a biological organism"; "You are an ego caught between the id and society"; "You are a spiritual being" are all statements about the person. *Person*, derived from *persona*, means "mask." Indeed, this public conceptual self is like a mask because it tends to hide a different, private conceptual self that is a repository of primitive self-appraisals, fantasies, and special interpretations of what the public sees. "I am really selfish"; "I am special"; "I can be great"; "I am unlovable"; "I am wonderful"; "I am worthless" are expressions of the private assessment of the self.

The public and private views overlap but do not coincide. The need to reconcile or conceal the discrepancies between them calls forth the strategies, "scripts," and fantasies—conscious or unconscious—that shape our lives and become the focus of most rational therapies. By "rational" I mean therapies that seek to clarify assumptions, conflicts, and misperceptions so as to reduce the dissonance and anxiety that stem from the need to hide the personal self. Psychoanalysis, Jungian Analytic Psychology, Transactional Analysis, Gestalt, and cognitive therapies address this domain in particular.

THE EMOTIONAL SELF

Anxiety, joy, anger, sadness, and desire constitute the second domain: the emotional self. At times this aspect seems closest to the core of our being, for nothing seems to be more completely our self than our emotions. Note that desire is included here, though it is not classifiable as an emotion per se. "I want" is a feeling similar to emotion, and it seems to originate from the same body location. The self that desires and the self that feels sadness and joy are phenomenologically the same. These feelings all constitute a self more vivid and compelling than the self of thought—and much more personal as well. While thoughts may seem alien, feelings seldom do.

Abreactive therapies (those that feature emotional catharsis) focus on this domain. We see this emphasis carried to its extreme in Primal therapy.

THE FUNCTIONAL SELF

The third domain of the self is the experience of our functional capacity. I know that I *do* things: I am aware of my acting, my capacity to affect the world around me in a concrete way. My body, with which I am identified by sensations and by my location in space, is the chief organ of the functional self, although unconscious processes of the mind may be experienced similarly.

Certain schools of thought focus on the wisdom and efficiency with which the body can function, surpassing consciously controlled thinking. Others, such as Psychosynthesis, use visualization techniques to widen the experience of the functional self. In this connection, Carl Simonton's work with cancer patients plus renewed interest in the "placebo effect" is drawing attention to the potential healing capacities resident in each person to do what the thinking self cannot. Such experiences convey the sense of a different self that has considerable power and sagacity. Even therapies focused on other domains may call on this "core self" more than they realize.

THE OBSERVING SELF

We have learned to interpret the thinking, feeling, and functioning selves as expressions of an object self. Thus, their activity supports and strengthens the object self and the mode of consciousness organized to serve it. But in considering the fourth domain, the observing self, we come to a phenomenon of a different order. The observing self is the transparent center, that which is aware. This fourth self is most personal of all, prior to thought, feeling, and action, for it experiences these functions. No matter what takes place, no matter what we experience, nothing is as central as the self that observes. In the face of this phenomenon, Descartes' starting point, "I think; therefore, I am," must yield to the more basic position, "I am aware; therefore, I am."

The most important fact about the observing self is that it is incapable of being objectified. The reader is invited to try to locate that self to establish its boundaries. The task is impossible; whatever we can notice or conceptualize is already an object of awareness, not awareness itself, which seems to jump a step back when we experience an object. Unlike every other aspect of experience—thoughts, emotions, desires, and functions — the observing self can be known but not located, not "seen."

The Yogic discipline of Ramana Maharshi prescribed the exercise of "Who am I?" to demonstrate that the observing self is not an object; it does not belong to the domains of thinking, feeling, or action:[1] "If I lost my arm, I would still exist, therefore, I am not my arm. If I could not hear, I would still exist. Therefore, I am not my hearing." And so on, until finally, "I am not this thought," which leads to a radically different experience of the self.

Western psychotherapy has yet to confront this paradox. The infinite regression of awareness, like two mirrors placed face to face, has largely been a subject for philosophers rather than scientists. The psychiatric and psychological literature refers to the observing self as "the observing ego," but does not explore the special nature of that "ego" and its implications for our understanding of the self.

The observing self is not part of the object world formed by our thoughts and sensory perception because, literally, it has no limits; everything else does. Thus, everyday consciousness contains a transcendent element that we seldom notice because that element is the very ground of our experience. The word *transcendent* is justified because if subjective consciousness — the observing self — cannot itself be observed but remains forever apart from the contents of consciousness, it is likely to be of a different order from everything else. Its fundamentally different nature becomes evident when we realize that the observing self is featureless; it cannot be affected by the world any more than a mirror can be affected by the images it reflects.

In the midst of the finite world is the "I," and it doesn't belong in that world. It is obviously different from the world but the difference is ignored. All else can be objectified, has limits and boundaries that can be described. All else is a segment of a world of fixed or relative dimensions. The observing self, however, is not like anything else we know.

Western science has ignored this transcendent element, assuming that the observer and the observed are phenomena of the same order. In contrast, the distinction between the observer and the observed is an important aspect of mysticism. It is emphasized in Vedanta and especially Sankhya philosophy, which distinguishes between Purusha, the Witness Soul, and Prakriti, all the phenomena of Nature. The following story, derived from the Vedantic literature, has many versions:

> A group of peasants forded a river. Afterward, concerned that someone might have been lost, the leader counted the group but omitted himself from the count. Each member then preceded to count the group in a similar fashion and arrived at a similar result. Dismayed that one of them was missing, the group spent many unhappy hours searching the river. An inquiring passer-by was able to solve the problem by suggesting to the leader that he count himself as well. The peasants were overjoyed to find that no one was missing and all proceeded on their way.

Like the peasant, Western psychology neglects to notice the one that counts. Until it does, progress will be delayed.

THE OBSERVING SELF
IN WESTERN PSYCHOTHERAPY

The failure to recognize the special importance of the observing self is all the more important because the development of Western psychotherapy has actually been based on the extraction of the observing self from that which is observed. With that separation, the observing self emerges with increasing clarity and stability, while the observed world of emotions, thoughts, and sensations becomes correspondingly less compelling, less dictatorial and unquestioned.

Other means of relieving psychological distress can be

employed; they have been practiced for thousands of years and continue to be practiced today. They include catharsis, insight, suggestion, alleviating guilt, adjustment in family systems, education, and confrontation. Nevertheless, I believe that the progressive clarification and strengthening of the observing self is the special contribution of Western psychotherapy, leading to the autonomy of the observing self from thought, emotion, and sensation, from conditioned perceptions and habitual reactions.

Mystical science has a technology for enhancing the observing self. The "Who am I?" exercise of Ramana Maharshi is perhaps the most straightforward approach to developing observer consciousness, but certain standard meditations pursue the same goal. These meditative techniques are remarkably similar to the basic psychoanalytic procedure. For example, *vipassana* (Theravadan Buddhist meditation) and *zazen* (Zen Buddhist meditation) both emphasize continuous observation of mind content. Students are instructed simply to watch the stream of thoughts and impressions going through their minds without making judgments or attempting to control it. Now compare Freud, writing about the fundamental technique of psychoanalysis:

> The treatment is begun by the patient being required to put himself in the position of an attentive and dispassionate self-observer . . .[2]
>
> We instruct the patient to put himself into a state of quiet, unreflecting self-observation, and to report to us whatever internal perceptions he is able to make — feelings, thoughts, memories — in the order in which they occur to him . . .[3]
>
> Act as though, for instance, you were a traveler sitting next to the window of a railway carriage and describing to someone inside the carriage the changing views which you see outside.[4]

Observing the processes of the mind is the basic technique of almost all modern psychotherapies, with the possible

exception of behavior modification.* Therapies that have
maturation and growth as their goals encourage patients to
distance themselves from thoughts and feelings in order to acquire choice and increase autonomy in the face of cognitive
and emotional reactions. This process is identical with the development and enhancement of the observing self. Many
purely cognitive techniques, such as writing down self-critical
thoughts and systematically evaluating them, can be understood as strengthening the observing self, extracting it from
processes in which it tends to be submerged.

As a further example, consider Gestalt Therapy, created
by Fritz Perls. This therapy can be understood as the effort
to extract the patient's observing self from the mass of thinking, fantasy, and automatic responses in which it is usually
hidden.

> If you are centered in yourself, then you don't adjust any-
> more — then, whatever happens becomes a passing parade
> and you assimilate, you understand, you are related to
> whatever happens.[6]

Perls taught that the important question for a patient to ask
is not "Why?" but "How?"

> If you ask *how* you look at the structure, you see what's
> going on now, a deeper understanding of the process. The
> *how* is all we need to understand how we or the world
> functions. The *how* gives us perspective, orientation.[7]

Thus, in this therapy, a patient who is suppressing tears
is not asked for the reasons motivating the defense but to
observe *how* he or she is managing to suppress the tears. For
example, the patient may become aware of his or her com-
pressed lips, or constricted breathing, or newly summoned
anger. Asking "How?" brings into awareness response patterns

---

*Although introspection is not a feature of behavior modification, there is evi-
dence that habit reversal is achieved by increasing self-awareness.[5]

that had functioned unconsciously and, therefore, automatically. The deautomatization of such responses results in a gain in freedom, both from the habitual responses themselves and through an increase in the scope and dominance of the observing self. "Why?" evokes thought; "How?" evokes observation.

Another technique of Gestalt Therapy is to give primary emphasis to the "now" (current sensations, emotions, desires, and perceptions) as opposed to fantasy, abstract thinking, or memories.

> *Now* covers all that exists. The past is no more, the future is not yet. *Now* includes the balance of being here, is experiencing, involvement, phenomena, awareness.[8]

Again, the intention is to increase awareness of what is being experienced. Such awareness is the operation of the observing self.

CONFUSED THEORY

It should be noted, however, that Perls did not realize that the awareness he endeavored to enhance was more basically a self than was the personality:

> Awareness covers, so to speak, three layers or three zones: awareness of the *self*, awareness of the *world*, and awareness of what's *between* — the intermediate zone of fantasy that prevents a person from being in touch with either himself or the world.[9]

In fact, the "person" who is "in touch with himself" *is* the observing self. Failure to equate awareness with the self results here, as elsewhere in confused theory. Such confusion is pervasive in the psychological and psychiatric literature dealing with the self.

The psychoanalytic literature occasionally makes reference to "the observing function of the ego" or "the observing ego." But although "the observing ego" is frequently mentioned, it is seldom discussed and its implications for an understanding of the self go unacknowledged. Only Miller and his colleagues address themselves to the topic at any length. Their article subsumes the "observing function" under a larger category of mental activities, namely, the ego.[10] The secondary status given to the observing self results in muddled statements such as the one by Waelder, which Miller et al. cite approvingly: "The function of self-observation connotes a self-objectification including the capacity to rise above the self."

The authors create further confusion by mixing up awareness, per se, with evaluation and criticism. Nevertheless, they make the useful point that "the observing function of the ego" undergoes development beginning at birth. They consider psychoanalysis to be of great value for completing this development and cite Sterba's proposition that an "observing ego" arises in the course of psychoanalytic treatment as a result of a "split" in the ego. The authors go on:

> We recognize that what Sterba called "dissociation within the ego" is not only highly desirable, but is also a prerequisite for insight psychotherapies. In large measure, the analyst's effort is directed toward enhancing such an observing function. He may do this in various ways, basically by using interpretations to free the patient's existing capacities or possibly by serving as a model for the patient with respect to ego activity.

Kohut has been developing a "psychology of the self," calling for a revision of psychoanalytic theory that would recognize the self as a superordinate concept, not just a function of the ego. But he too makes the typical and crucial error of ignoring the observing self or confusing it with the contents of observation. In the end, Kohut's "self" is another concept of the mind, a psychic "structure" with a psychic "location," analogous to an object:

> The self is a structure within the mind since (a) it is cathected with instinctual energy and (b) it has continuity in time, i.e., it is enduring. Being a psychic structure, the self has, furthermore, also a psychic location. To be more specific, various—and frequently inconsistent—self representations are present not only in the id, the ego, and the superego, but also within a single agency of the mind. There

may, for example, exist contradictory conscious and preconscious self representations — e.g., of grandiosity and
inferiority—side by side, occupying either delimited loci
within the realm of the ego or sectorial positions of that
realm of the psyche in which id and ego form a continuum. The self then, quite analogous to the representations
of objects, is a content of the mental apparatus.[11]

Kohut perceives the need to make the self central but is
caught within the existing paradigm, which does not recognize awareness as the primary source of self-experience.
Awareness is a phenomenon in its own right; the contents are
secondary. For this reason it is a crucial error to regard the
observing self, which is the center and source of our personal
existence, as "a content of the mental apparatus" because it
transcends all content. Western psychology has yet to cope
with this fact and the psychiatric literature, with rare excep-
tions, simply ignores it.

In this connection, two recent attempts at understanding the nature of the observing self are worth noting. Both
try to take into account the observing self's unique characteristic of invisibility and the infinite regression that occurs
when one pursues it. At the same time, both illustrate the difficulty of encompassing the observing self within the usual
frame of reference.

C. O. Evans, after reviewing previous philosophical attempts to solve the problem, proposed a solution in terms of
cognitive psychology.[12] He began by introducing and defining the term *unprojected consciousness*: "I give the name
'unprojected consciousness' to those elements of consciousness that together make up the background of consciousness
when attention is paid to the object."[13]

He then equates the observing self with unprojected
consciousness:

If the self *is* unprojected consciousness, then the self can
no more become an object of attention and remain subject
than an element of unprojected consciousness can become

an object of attention and remain an element of unprojected consciousness.[14]

In other words, what we experience as the observing self
is the experience of those elements that are not being at-
tended to at any one time. In making this equation, Evans
has performed a sleight of hand. Because it can be said that
the observing self forms the background to all experience,
and objects in the foreground of perception all have a background, he equates the background of experience and the
background of perceptual objects. However, the two back-
grounds are different. As he indicates in his definition, unprojected consciousness consists of elements. We can infer or
demonstrate the existence of these elements simply by shifting attention to them; they constitute what Freud termed the
preconscious. In contrast, however, the observing self has no
elements, no features whatsoever. It is not a question of a
searchlight illuminating one area while another is dark, but of
the nature of the light itself.

Another attempt to deal with the observing function
demonstrates the futility of approaching the problem through
an equation with known elements. Gordon Globus explains
the observing self — which he calls the "I" — as the mental actions that distinguish a meaningful world of objects.[15] Although he starts out by recognizing the featureless, ungraspable
character of awareness and categorically separates it from
everything else in the world of experience ("an analytic sin-
gularity"), he then proceeds to talk of the "I" as disappearing
when the subject/object distinction disappears, as in certain
meditation states of "unbroken," "holistic," "undivided"
consciousness. Clearly, at this point, Globus is no longer talk-
ing about awareness per se, but about the object self and the
mental activity of discriminating objects. Awareness cannot be
absent where there is consciousness. It *is* consciousness.The
activity of discriminating is different; it is mundane, it can be

observed, and even if some activities are subconscious their effects can be observed as contents of consciousness. In the higher meditative states, contents cease but awareness remains.

Such attempts at explanation do not work because they are based on object consciousness, and the observing self is not an object; it transcends the sensate world. Consequently, Western psychology continues to miss the significance of the observing self, and its theories of the self remain confused.

THE KNOWING OF AWARENESS

When we consider the radically different nature of the observing self, it is apparent that some mode of knowing other than the senses or intellect is involved in that phenomenon. The senses and intellect provide content: sounds, vision, touch, ideas, memories, fantasies. But the observing self is outside content and thus outside intellect and sensation. It follows that a different type of knowing is involved, one we must designate as intuitive, or direct, knowing — knowing by being that which is known. We *are* awareness, and that is why we cannot observe it; we cannot detach ourselves from it because it is the core experience of self.

I will use an analogy to illustrate how direct knowing might take place and what its relationship to ordinary thought could be. Consider a pond that borders on and is continuous with the ocean. Our awareness, the observing self, is the surface of the pond. Thoughts, feelings, and other mental activities are like splashes and ripples in the water, as if small stones were being tossed in from the shore. When such activity subsides, the pond is smooth, still, and reflective; at such times the observing self is enhanced, becomes prominent, and is the major dimension of consciousness. At other times, when thought has transformed the surface into a mass of waves and ripples, awareness seems to have vanished and consciousness contains only the patterns of disturbance in the water. In such a situation there is no need to postulate an outside observer to experience the stillness and the ripples. There need be no experiencing agency because the experience is the state of stillness or ripples, as the case may be.

We can then address the question, "Why are thoughts and feelings observed but awareness known directly?" The answer is that the ripples are local phenomena but water per se is not. The activity occurs against the background of stillness and through the medium of water.

When the water becomes still, and the quiet extends to a sufficient depth, the pond begins to resonate with the longer phase pulsations originating from the ocean. When stillness and activity are in proper balance, the state of the pond reflects the subtle rhythyms that are ordinarily obscured and confused by surface ripples.

Using such a model, we can understand how unconsciousness and death would affect awareness. When all activity ceases completely, awareness cannot be known intellectually in the particular locale (the pond) that is the individual person because there would be no localizing activity at all.

To translate back into the terms of mystical science: through appropriate teaching, object self (local) motivations and their corresponding form of consciousness can subside and cease to dominate perception. Then the person becomes aware of the subtler, deeper currents that reflect and permeate reality. When this takes place, people experience their continuity and identity with that larger activity to which is given various names: Self, Tao, Truth, Brahman, or God.

The analogy of the pond and the ocean is limited because it is three-dimensional and cannot show us the transcendent character of awareness as compared to thought contents. Thus, it is not an explanation of awareness but a way of appreciating how awareness and intuitive knowing might operate, how they might be possible. The analogy is also useful in understanding the reciprocal relationship of awareness and mental activity.

Although I call the observing self transcendent, there is not necessarily anything esoteric or religious about it. Understanding the observing self is a matter of widening our perspective to include something that has always been there but has been difficult to acknowledge because it does not fit the framework to which we are accustomed.

THE DEVELOPMENT OF THE OBSERVING SELF

Many theories have been proposed to account for the effects of psychotherapy and, undoubtedly, many factors can be found to correlate with various levels of change. However, as we have seen, the therapeutic importance of the development of the observing self has not been emphasized. Even "the observing function of the ego" is not given much attention despite the fact that the techniques of most psychotherapies revolve around it. The observing self has occupied a peripheral position in the psychotherapeutic literature because of its unique nature, which does not fit into the contemporary materialistic paradigm. Miller and his colleagues, who come closest to acknowledging the significance of the observing self, do not mention its transcendent quality. However, they do discuss the diminished observing function found in neurosis, psychosis, character disorder, or "defective ego-apparatus" and this diminished capacity is interpreted as taking place for defensive reasons (to prevent awareness) either on an acute, ad hoc basis or, more chronically, as a character trait resulting from faulty identification or pervasive defensive style. They postulate some people's lack of the observing function may be genetic or the result of a very early physical or psychological trauma.

If we take a wider, evolutionary perspective, however, it is not unreasonable to suggest that even the normal observing self represents only a partial development compared to what might be possible, even for those who have undergone formal psychoanalysis or long-term psychotherapy. Consider Miller's and his colleagues' description of the "final" stage of development of the observing function:

> . . . there develops that stage of observation which is the prime concern of the writers. It involves the observation of ego processes in connection with inner as well as outer events in dynamic interactions. In this the concern is with the observation of drive, affect, defense, expression, and the participation of the ego in these. It is an integrated observation of causal relationships within the ego. That is, it is concerned with causal association of "I perceive such and such, I react in such a way, which then leads me to thus and so."[16]

As I will show, the domain of the observing self can be extended to include cultural assumptions and socially approved self-deceit. Judging by the mystical literature, the most basic assumptions of our world view, those challenged now by the advance of theoretical physics, can also come under the gaze of the observing self so that they cease to operate as controlling, limiting factors of mental life. The "final" phase of development of the observing self probably cannot be conceptualized.

Again, although the theoretical foundation of psychotherapy makes little reference to the developmental potential of the observing self, psychoanalysis and psychotherapy can be viewed as procedures that facilitate this development and therein lies their unique contribution. How does such development come about? Clinical evidence indicates that too much or too little affect interferes with the process:

> In order to have a sense of conviction about what is being observed, there must be affective experience, for insuffi-

ciency of affect results in sterile intellectualization, a condition which is ineffective for the development of insight. On the other hand, flooding with affect overwhelms perceptual, cognitive and integrative functions.[17]

This statement echoes the emphasis in mystical science on the need for balance, harmony, and moderation in the emotional life. Further parallels to mysticism are evident in the Miller et al. discussion of the means whereby the observing function is "split off" from the "experiencing ego." They emphasize the use of interpretations to identify defensive patterns of behavior (self-centered motivations). Furthermore, they indicate that the analyst should model the proper attitude of observation, as well as affective balance, to feature an interest in learning and a willingness to be surprised by new information. The therapist should be able to transmit to the patient the calm that comes from the absence of fear.

In all these areas, there is no substitute for the real thing. A therapist whose own development of the observing self has not brought him or her to the desired stage will not be able to transmit it to the patient. Similarly, the mystical literature indicates that teachers must teach by means of what they can transmit *because of what they have become*. To help a patient enhance the observing self, the therapist must have accomplished that task first. This requirement probably explains why therapeutic techniques used by themselves yield only limited and temporary results. It follows that uncovering the patient's past need not be helpful if the observing self has not been established with sufficient clarity. The extraction and enhancement of the observing self are essential to providing autonomy from emotional responses that otherwise render knowledge of the past useless.

I have suggested that the basic activity of psychotherapy, as practiced in the West, is to extract the observing self from the contents of consciousness. Once we do that, we will be able to locate ourselves in the observer instead of the contents—those patterns of emotions, thoughts, and fantasies responsible for our pain. By dis-identifying with automatic sequences we lessen their impact and provide free space in which to choose an appropriate response. Thus, we achieve autonomy where previously we were overwhelmed and helpless. Anxiety, depression, and rage, even if not abolished, become restricted in their scope and attenuated. By identifying with the observing self, we can make a more realistic assessment of ourselves and our situation, permitting more effective and creative behavior. The following anecdote illustrates how this change in "location" was positively communicated to a patient:

A woman I had been seeing in once-a-week psychotherapy entered my office almost frantic with distress, proclaiming anxiously that she was about "to go to pieces." My usual approach would have been to listen, draw out some explanation of the precipitating circumstances, and bring into awareness the repressed emotions, wishes, or ideas that presumably were the bases for her acute symptoms. This way of proceeding would most likely have been of some help. What actually happened was that I began to smile, feeling amused. The woman's distress was genuine by all the criteria customarily used in such situations. She was not prone to having crises and her statements were not hysterically exaggerated. Yet I found myself smiling. Her situation seemed funny to me because I perceived her as being in no actual danger, but completely caught up in the contents of her mind, identifying with the commotion she was reporting, forgetting that *she* was observing *it*. Speaking metaphorically, it was as if the patient were standing on a hilltop overlooking the ocean and on seeing large waves crashing far out to sea had become fearful that she would drown, forgetting where she actually was.

The woman suddenly became aware of my facial expression, stopped, and indignantly demanded the reason for my "unfeeling" smile in response to her desperation. Her question made me smile even more broadly, and I actually began to laugh. She stared at me in disbelief, and then a look of outrage took possession of her face. However, in the midst of her rising anger, despite herself, she started to smile, too. "Damn you!" she exclaimed and began to laugh. We laughed together for a long while. The desperate air of crisis, the emergency, the impending breakdown vanished in that laughter like fog evaporating in the sun. The "going to pieces" never happened.

This is not an example of a new therapy; explanations based on a variety of theories can be constructed for the incident. However, as far as I can tell, my response was the result of the special perspective on the observing self I had acquired from my studies of mysticism. I saw the situation differently and was able to communicate that new perspective to the patient by my laughter and the attitude that accompanied it. One might argue that the standard exploratory approach would have increased the patient's awareness of her repressed impulses and therefore would have yielded a more important gain than did the resolution of the crisis, which my unexpected response accomplished. This may be true, except that the effect of the hour seemed to be more than temporary relief. The woman's psychotherapeutic progress took a leap forward in succeeding sessions. I think a different kind of learning took place, involving taking distance from anxiety and observing it rather than identifying with it. This learning was useful to her.

A FLEXIBLE AWARENESS

Numerous investigations have shown that our capacity to process information has limits; for example, it is unusual for a person to be able to remember more than seven random digits spoken in sequence. Similarly, it is hard to "pay attention" to more than one thing at a time. At a more general level, thought activity diminishes sensation, and vice versa; the two ordinarily do not increase together but change inversely. A similar reciprocal relationship exists between the observing self and the contents of consciousness: as one becomes more prominent, the other recedes. This may explain why healthy functioning calls for the capacity to increase or decrease the observing self. On the one hand, heightening the observing self reduces the intensity of affect, of obsessive thinking, and of automatic response patterns, thus providing the opportunity for modification and control, for increased mastery. On the other hand, maximum richness of sensory experience — as in orgasm — or maximum efficiency in solving intellectual problems — as in making calculations or playing chess — cannot be achieved by a person who is unable to relinquish the observing self so as to invest maximum energy in the perceptual apparatus or cognitive process. However, for most people it is the observing self that needs development.

In using the perspective of the observing self, Western psychology is not obliged to relinquish any of its gains. It is a matter of including and restoring to primacy what is already central and dominant in our experience, the basis for experience itself. As in the parable of the peasant who did not count himself, awareness of awareness makes the difference.

OBSERVING CULTURAL ASSUMPTIONS

It is important for patients and therapists alike to be able to observe the defenses and affects related to the object self instead of being caught up in them. Such observation results in increased freedom of choice, increased autonomy, and a wider scope of comprehension. But defenses and emotions are not the only mind content to be observed. Most people are immersed in other mental processes, more fundamental mind patterns that operate without their being aware of them. The observing self can be extracted from these processes too, yielding further gains in autonomy and clarity.

The assumptions of our culture form one layer of such mental processes. These assumptions dominate a wide area: what is good and what is evil, the nature of human beings, the meaning of life, and what is real and what is unreal. Insofar as we take these assumptions for granted we are bound by them, caught by them. In psychotherapy, these basic assumptions tend to remain unscrutinized because the therapist shares them. The therapist cannot extend the domain of the patient's observing self to areas in which the therapist is also captive.

Consider the value placed on unselfishness in our culture. For the ordinary person, unselfishness is understood to consist in doing things for others — donating money, helping someone in other ways, or relinquishing one's share to another. We seldom notice that such behavior may be a type of deferred gain, a means of acquisition. If the recipient knows the donor, the donor can expect to receive gratitude, admiration, and praise. Even if the gift is anonymous, the giver may gain self-esteem and mentally add to his or her account with heaven, making another payment on the celestial homestead. However, most people are oblivious to this aspect of their behavior. It is interesting, indeed, to note patients' astonishment when you point out that their righteous anger at someone's "ingratitude" toward them betrays the commercial nature of the transaction: they gave in expectation of a return. Such an analysis is not fanciful or semantic — it is concretely true. Commerce is commerce, even if it is called "self-sacrifice" or "altruism." The acquisitive mode operates with any commodity: money, praise, self-esteem, virtue — anything. Only through awareness, through observation of the underlying pattern, can the observing self gain independence from the domain of self-interest.

As we have seen in discussing sincerity of intention, this laying bare of socially sanctioned greed is characteristic of mystical science. But in psychotherapy it is most unusual, because therapists are the products of a culture that has not yet extended its observation to these levels. Self-interest is the basis of our economic system, religions, and international relations, and it extends to the therapeutic contract itself. We pursue activities to *gain* happiness, satisfaction, creative pleasures, sensual enjoyment, power, prestige, self-esteem, and so on.

Because therapists tend to accept the assumption that self-interest inevitably is the basis for social life and individual activity, they cannot help their patients escape from the consequences of such motivations, especially when neither therapists nor patients understand the source of those consequences. Here again, the mystical tradition can benefit, not by providing new techniques, but by widening the perspective and understanding of therapists. For mystical science does have an answer to the question, "What other motivation could there be that is not reducible to self-interest?" That answer is: serving the requirements of the task at hand.

SERVING THE TASK

When we speak of doing a job well, for its own sake, we refer to a shift in motivation in which we give the needs of the job precedence over our own wishes. We recognize that the proper accomplishment of the task may *call for* a certain amount and type of effort. For example, in writing this book, I may be aware that a certain passage isn't quite the way it should be; it is not complete, not finished. I can get by with it; it will do, but I feel that it is not the way it deserves to be and am pulled to meet its requirements, even if no one else notices the difference. The pull is not a compulsion but a recognition that the task is not complete *in its own terms*. I may decide that I am unable to do what is required or that it will not be worth the time or effort needed but, nevertheless, the perception is clear — something more is called for.

Doing what is needed instead of what you might prefer to do is a choice that occurs in a wide range of situations — intellectual, mechanical, artistic, or interpersonal. In all such instances, the experience may be described as surrendering to the task, but it is a surrender in which the person is active and guided at the same time.

Psychotherapists are likely to have this experience during a "good" hour, when everything seems to conduct itself well, everything "flows." The therapist responds to the situation as its servant, acting in perfect synchrony with the patient's cues, following a subtle path that seems to carry as much as lead. Self-interest and self-concern disappear when "what-is-called-for" takes over. The experience is memorable, "magical," successful in its result and very satisfying to patient and therapist alike. It is high art.

Zen Buddhism focuses on task-serving behavior in its emphasis on the Now. Although this idea is often presented in an esoteric format, Nowness is experienced when you "just do it," forsaking self-interest in favor of responding to the immediate needs of the situation. Consider the following description of the "self-less" Sage by Huang Po, a ninth-century Zen master:

when all action is dictated purely by place and circumstances . . .

so they were called "Sages" who, abandoning learning, have come to rest in spontaneity (wu wei).[18]

The shift to task-oriented behavior changes the mode of consciousness. With the shift in consciousness, different dimensions emerge and come into focus, while others fade away and disappear. Fundamental reality becomes more accessible to perception. Thus, service is functional, not moral.

Serving the task creates the conditions for a different experience of the self and the world, but it does not represent obliteration of the object self. Rather, serving the task requires a combination of the object and the receptive modes of consciousness, both operating in balance with the observing self. The object mode is necessary for effective action; the receptive mode for sensitivity to subtle information from the environment pertaining to the requirements of the task, moment by moment. An enhanced observing self prevents the dominance of either mode by establishing an optimum degree of detachment, which reduces the influence of anxiety generated by the object self and prevents excessive absorption in the receptive mode. The quality of that balanced state is conveyed, perhaps, by Yeats's description of creative activity:

Like a long-legged fly upon the stream
His mind moves upon silence.[19]

SERVING THE TASK AND
THE PROBLEM OF MEANING

Patients frequently complain that their lives lack meaning. Although their complaints may be based on neurotic problems such as an interference with the capacity to love or to experience intimacy, they may also be describing a life that is meaningless because it is self-centered, motivated by the demands of the object self. It is not surprising that such a life would eventually feel meaningless. For one thing, the object self can never be satisfied because its wish for permanence and for possession of all it desires can never be achieved. For another, at the end of the road stands death to take away all possessions, everything cherished by the object self. A life devoted to self-interest is futile, lacking in meaning, and persons who complain of it may be reflecting an accurate perception of their lives, rather than neuroses.

There is no solution to the problem of meaning except to transcend the motivations of the object self. The path to that transcendence is service — real service, which means serving the task and, ultimately, serving what mystics call the Truth. In terms of the pond analogy, when the local agitation (object self) subsides sufficiently, the pond responds to the currents that link it to the ocean. When people are able to reduce the demands of the object self they can respond to a larger flow. By aligning themselves with that flow, they not only act to further the current, but they can experience themselves as continuous with the ocean rather than restricted to the pond. With the experience of the larger identity, fear subsides and meaning is perceived.

Psychotherapists can hardly say all this to their patients or bring that evolution to completion, but such a perspective can improve their responses and their guidance of the therapy. They can understand the patient's complaints and evaluate them in a wider context. At suitable times they can intervene to extract the patient's observing self from the tight enclosure of self-centered thinking, creating the possibility of a deeper and wider knowledge of self and world. Psychotherapists must understand this perspective if they are to deal with the problem of meaning. After all, it helps to make the correct diagnosis in treating an illness. At the least, one can recognize that a disorder of motivation is involved, not a natural condition to be accepted as the inevitable fate of human beings.

An example of the usefulness of the mystical perspective for psychotherapy is that of a woman in her forties who had been suffering from severe periods of depression, which occurred every year at about the same time despite many years of psychoanalysis. The depression was characterized by a profound feeling of the meaninglessness of her life and of life in general. Typically, she would deal with her problem by taking to her bed and spending weeks in blank despair.

I responded to her complaint by suggesting that her sense of meaninglessness might be a valuable and correct perception of the world on one level. I pointed out that great mystics, like Saint Theresa and John of the Cross had all experienced "the dark night of the soul" and had come through it to a new position of strength and vision that permitted them to function with outstanding effectiveness in the everyday world. I suggested to my patient that she "go with" the feeling of meaninglessness instead of fighting it, and learn what it could teach her. I proposed that she adopt the attitude of a researcher and make the most of what might be an opportunity to progress in her development.

She listened with increasing interest and excitement. The concept made sense to her and immediately relieved her of some of her suffering because she had thought her perception was pathological. When she came for her next appointment a few days later, she was markedly better. In succeeding days, as she replaced her helpless attitude with one of positive interest toward her psychological state, her sense of overall meaninglessness faded and she was able to examine the actual meaninglessness of certain aspects of the world and her own life. She had perceived this for many years, but had suppressed the perception to avoid conflict with others on whom she depended.

SERVING THE TRUTH

Many people experience the "selfless" mode in their everyday lives but do not recognize its unique and important character. They do not see the connection between the ethic of "doing a job well for its own sake" and the mystical admonition to "serve Truth for its own sake." But according to mystical science, after reducing the dominance of self-interest, people may be able to perceive, intuitively, the larger "transcendent" task. This perception enables them "to serve the will of God," a phrase much misused by those in whom self-interest is still very active. In this connection, Rabia, the Sufi saint, declared:

Oh Lord:
 If I worship you from fear of hell, cast me
  into hell.
 If I worship you from desire for paradise,
  deny me paradise.[20]

Purposely dramatic, the statement, which highlights the self-interest of many "spiritual" people, is intended to bring such self-centeredness under observation in order to lessen its effect on consciousness.

It is logical that human beings, in the first phase of their lives, should focus on possessiveness and self-preservation. The human organism is needed to convey life and to evolve it, something it can do only by first surviving. At the same time, human beings have connections with reality that go beyond the dimensions apparent to their senses and intellect — they are part of a much larger field. Just as initially one had to serve the object self for the human organism to live, one next has to serve the larger field of which it is a component for the human race, as a whole, to survive and evolve.

I have focused on the issue of the observing self because it is central to the work of both psychotherapy and mystical science. The issue of selflessness and service illustrates the importance of extending the scope of the observing self to include within its domain the blind spots of our culture, the assumptions and self-deceits made invisible by group acceptance. One of these assumptions has relegated the observing self to a peripheral position or a nonexistent status, with the result that a comprehensive self psychology has not yet been developed.

If mystics are correct, through properly guided self-observation we can begin our escape from the circle of self-centeredness to a new realm of freedom and a new source of knowledge — in fulfillment of our developmental journey. The perception of that evolutionary task, and the self integral to it, is not possible to the restricted awareness of the ordinary person who, in this respect, may be said to be asleep.

9

The Trance of Ordinary Life

Although as adults we seem to deal with the world in concrete, practical terms, fully occupied with the business at hand, introspection demonstrates that much of the time we dwell on abstract, tangential thoughts and fantasies. When we suddenly shift from such preoccupations to a full, vivid awareness of the world, the contrast is so great we may describe ourselves as "coming to" or "waking up." Correspondingly, someone deeply absorbed in thoughts and fantasies is said to be "in a trance." It is precisely the trance aspect of normal waking consciousness that I wish to discuss.

One immediate benefit of adopting the perspective of the observing self is that we can begin to detect and understand the problem posed by this state of human consciousness, which usually goes unnoticed. The predilection of people to be preoccupied with imaginings, to confine their attention to narrow segments of reality, is a tendency with which mystical science is much concerned but which psychotherapy deals with only indirectly. I call it the trance of ordinary life.

As shown in the preceding chapter, reflection leads to the understanding that our center is in the observing self, and that all our other "selves" are peripheral to that center, subject to its observation, detachable and transient. To think of ourselves only as objects is to distort reality, to construct a key fantasy that has far-reaching consequences. For example, belief in an object self is accompanied by fantasies of loss and dissolution, which spawn anxiety, which in turn leads to further fantasies that take their form from the dramatic world of dependency in which our basic learning takes place. On the stage of the childhood theater a small and vulnerable child seduces and coerces powerful parental figures to ensure the nourishment, attention, and love only they can provide. Strategies of fear and control rule a warfare of the mind, a drama in which all persons are forced into preformed, stereotyped roles. As a result we arrive at adulthood participating in a life of fantasy far more pervasive than we realize, a life like an underground river, flowing behind our conscious thoughts, shaping and moving them with hidden power. That current of fantasy is the basis of the unrecognized trance in which we spend most of our lives.

THE DYNAMICS OF HYPNOSIS

In technical usage, the word *trance* refers to the behavior of someone who has been hypnotized and is not responding normally: awareness is restricted, attention is fixed, and behavior appears to be automatic, in response to suggestions and commands. The overall impression is that the person is in a type of sleep, since he or she seems to be internally preoccupied and oblivious to most external stimuli. Thus, trance seems to be a special state of consciousness. But, in fact, ordinary day-to-day preoccupations can produce brief periods of behavior that have somewhat similar qualities, though they are much less intense.

In ordinary life, as well as under the influence of hypnosis, trance can be understood as a loss of context. Most of the time we function within a conceptual framework of which we are only marginally aware, a context that places us in time, geographic area, culture, and social role and provides self-definition. Thus, as I sit at my desk and write, or as I talk to a friend or drive a car, my activity is given meaning and direction by a loose backdrop of concepts and memories that place me in the flow of experience. This subsidiary frame upon which my psychological orientation depends has been termed "the frame of reference" or "frame of activation" by R. W. White, who hypothesized that in hypnosis the frame of reference is "contracted."[1]

Continuing White's analysis, R. Shor proposed the term "generalized reality-orientation" instead of "frame of reference" and extended White's hypothesis into a series of postulates about the hypnotic state.[2] He suggested that three dynamic factors are involved in a hypnotic trance and that their relative intensity determines the characteristic of the trance as it varies from person to person. In considering these characteristics one by one, I intend to show that they apply not only to the hypnotic trance state but also to ordinary consciousness.

The first factor concerns "the generalized reality-orientation," which

> supports, interprets and gives meaning to all experiences . . . In normal waking life, even where special aspects of the generalized reality-orientation are in central focus, the rest of it is in close communication at all times. When close communication is lost, the resultant state of mind may be designated as trance. Any state in which the generalized reality-orientation has faded to relatively nonfunctional awareness may be termed a trance state.[3]

Considered this way, trance is not confined to hypnosis. Similar states of absorption are associated with fatigue, drugs, and certain aspects of creative work. However, the intensity of the trance, or its depth, depends on how completely the generalized reality-orientation has faded away.

The second factor is that of role-taking. Shor postulates that subjects of hypnosis take on the characteristics of a hypnotized person, as they are perceived in his or her culture.* Such role-taking represents a usually unconscious compliance that nevertheless directs the subject's behavior. In this regard, White has shown that hypnotic subjects are characterized by "goal-directed striving," and Sarbin has labeled the compliance "as-if" behavior, noting that as-if phenomena are not confined to hypnosis:

> We noted the apparent relationship between role-taking of the drama and role-taking in hypnosis. Mr. Arbuthnot, the actor, in taking the part of Hamlet, acts *as if* he is Hamlet and not Mr. Arbuthnot. The hypnotic subject acts *as if* he is an automaton (if automaticity is included in his role perception) . . . The *as-if* formulation may be seen not only in the drama, in hypnosis, but in fantasy, play, and, in fact, all imaginative behavior.[5]

This point is of particular importance, for I wish to suggest that ordinary persons behave almost all the time "as if" they were what their parents or their culture (the generalized parent) explicitly and implicitly instructed them to be.

Unconsciously, human beings strive to please and win the approval of fantasized parental figures by fulfilling their implied wishes. When these hidden instructions can be made conscious and articulated in psychotherapy, the patient's observing self is enhanced and increased autonomy results. But, as I emphasized in the preceding chapter, awareness of the more fundamental instructions — the basic assumptions of our civilized world — is more difficult to achieve. These controlling assumptions are so pervasive and axiomatic that even the most rebellious, outwardly defiant individuals do not notice them, to say nothing of academically trained psychotherapists. Mystical science attempts to dissolve this prison of assumptions, whereas most psychotherapy tends to remain within it.

*See also Martin Orne's experimental demonstration of "demand characteristics" in the hypnotic situation.[4]

In Shor's description, the third dynamic governing the hypnotic trance is "archaic involvement," which is determined by

a) the extent to which during hypnosis archaic object relationships are formed onto the person of the hypnotist; b) the extent to which a specific hypnotic "transference" relationship is formed onto the person of the hypnotist; c) the extent to which the core of the subject's personality is involved in the hypnotic process.[6]

Archaic involvement is motivated by dependency wishes, wishes to have parents who will provide, protect, comfort, and nourish. These wishes are structured into fantasies that result in an orientation toward reward and punishment, approval, protection, awe, and deference. In psychotherapy the therapist helps clarify such fantasies by laying bare the motivations that drive an activity and by examining the way in which a patient distorts the relationship with the therapist.

In ordinary life situations, dependency wishes are expressed in adult roles that emphasize helplessness or power, roles from which a person looks up to or down on other human beings. Certain behavioral cues reveal the presence of these dependency fantasies. For example, complaints carry a message: "I am not happy and someone should do something about it." The accusatory mode points the finger and says, "*You* are bad" (not I). In the dependency context, people demand adult freedom while disclaiming adult responsibilities. For example, people break laws in ways that are accepted by their peers, but express contempt and hate for the lawlessness of others. Dependency is perhaps most visible in the piles of beer and whiskey bottles, tin cans, paper bags, and refuse left in parks and waysides to mark the passing of human beings. Such messing of the world takes place in a fantasy of childhood freedom and privilege, of five-year-old egocentricity. Just as hypnosis reflects the combination of narrowed attention and dependency on the hypnotist, the "trance" of everyday life reflects the channeling of attention into the unconscious fantasies of childhood.

Traditionally, hypnotic trance is associated with dramatic commands or gestures; the classical tableau is of a dominant male hypnotist and a passive female subject. But given the ubiquitous character of archaic childhood fantasies, trance does not require such drama. Trance should be considered a capacity present in everyone. It exists when one hears a suggestion in the context of a dependency fantasy; the suggestion may be from an individual, an institution, or from the media serving the culture at large. Weitzenhoffer comments:

> All bona fide (spontaneous) responses to suggestions are associated, *ipso facto*, with a hypnotic or trance state. From this standpoint there is no longer any distinction between "waking" and "hypnotic" suggestions, or if one prefers, between extra and intrahypnotic suggestions. To respond adequately to a suggestion is to be hypnotized.[7]

Weitzenhoffer's comment is based on the work of Milton Erickson, whose ability to bring about trance through subtle, indirect means is legendary. Even when Erickson did not seem to be performing a hypnotic induction, his subjects went into trance nevertheless. He relied on suggestions tailored to the presenting behavior of the subject, thus fitting into the fantasies that formed the background to the subject's style and current preoccupations. Jay Haley, another interpreter of Erickson's work, has proposed that entering a state of trance solves the double-bind message that says, "Obey this command, spontaneously!" The development of the trance permits one to be both unconsciously obedient and, on the surface, "spontaneous" and "independent."[8]

THE PRISON OF FANTASY

I suggest that just as the hypnotic subject complies with the hypnotist and the implied characteristics of the relationship between them, so the ordinary person constantly complies with demands of the internal parental figures from whom he or she hopes to wrest love, praise, power, and security by obeying their wishes — in short, by being "good." Like the hypnotic subject, such compliance is unconscious, contained in fantasies.

In psychotherapy, it is possible to bring into awareness such a controlling fantasy, freeing the observing self from the area in question. With that increased freedom the automatized compliance and the trance associated with the fantasy can be broken. The result is closer contact with immediate reality, heightened perception of surroundings and people, and increased satisfaction in daily existence. The patient may describe the change as "waking up from a dream."

Readers may be skeptical and tend to dismiss this description of pervasive fantasy as an exaggeration, a type of psychiatric overkill. After all, most of the time we are not fantasizing about our parents. Indeed, we may not think about them at all for long periods of time. However, close examination of the origins of our desires and goals, of our anxieties, depressions, elation, and anger, reveals that most of our imaginings about ourselves and the world are in fact childhood fantasies.

For example, it is not uncommon for a person to discover in psychotherapy that a primary goal of his or her work has been to achieve fame or, at least, admiration from friends. If the wish is explored, it may be found to lead to a fantasy in which he or she is surrounded by admiring smiling faces and feels secure, loved, and accepted. Such feelings lead, in turn, to deeper images of an unlovable self and disapproving parents or peers — fantasies of isolation and rejection. These fantasies may be a long way from waking consciousness, but the "desire" for success may take place with the mind's eye fixed on this inner movie composed of dramatic scenes in which he or she moves through a predetermined role. Much, if not most, of our activity consists of the unknowing enactment of these dramas. In this way, we tend to live our lives compliant to hidden dreams.

To take another example, people who work as if "driven" also have their mental vision focused on an imaginary scene of one sort or another. They give the outer world only partial attention; it serves as background to the fantasy that absorbs their consciousness. In this case, the fantasy is a belief that without continuous, harsh effort they will lapse into their natural, slothful state and lose all hope of happiness. As psychotherapists are well aware, this is not just a concept; such persons are likely to have constructed an actual image of their uncontrolled self, a caricature of the balky, messy, "naughty" child. They can usually draw the image if asked to do so. Furthermore, the imagined child exists in a landscape of disapproving, rejecting, or absent people. The controlling fantasy hovers vigilantly, waiting to punish any deviation from the defensive strategies it has inspired.

Fantasies are not only associated with psychopathology; they form the guiding backdrop for much of everyday living. Most persons who stop to observe their thoughts, concerns, and desires become aware that they pass most of their time in a sleep of fantasy — a trance — even if, at the same time, they are consciously pursuing practical goals.

As a sphere of ordinary life in which such imaginings are pervasive, consider how male and female roles have been tyranically imposed by children's fantasies incorporated into an adult culture. The castrating bitch; the pure, unattainable maiden; the sadistic, leering brute; the selfish baby; the emotional, dumb female; and the stoical, strong male — these distorted images are patterns to which identities are shaped. Each such fantasy has its consequences in the practical world. A woman complains that if she doesn't go to bed with a man, he will leave her, and if she does, he will leave her soon afterward anyway. A man complains that women "trap" him, luring him with pleasure and attention, only later to reveal insatiable demands. Men and women are unaware of the extent to which fantasy controls their actions because the images are so interwoven with ordinary thought that they go unnoticed. In psychotherapy, as the observing self extends its domain, the fantasies supporting these stereotypes become more clear. A man may discover that he tends to see women as young goddesses when they are distant and as aging jailers when they are close. A woman may come to see that in fantasy she has given a man paternal power, strength, and generosity in order to serve her dependency needs and then, confronted with his own, has seen him as a greedy child, uncaring.

Although we recognize descriptions of these fantasies and may be bored at hearing them once again, we can still be startled to find them operating in ourselves, producing anger, depression, infidelity, and silence. The subtler effects of hidden fantasy results in familiar complaints, although their cause cannot be readily seen: "You're not really there!" "I'm just an object to you." "You don't really see me!"

We find it somewhat easier to understand the influence of fantasy in our sexual relationships than in other areas of our lives — for example, in the domain of power and ambition. But if we study the goal of power we see that regardless of whether one is aiming to achieve it through money, sex, magic, or "spiritual" means, the desire for power is energized by a fantasy. In this case, the nature of the fantasy can often be elicited by asking, "After you have the power, what then?" The answer, usually in an image, may reveal a wish for control over loss or death, or for reassurance against another fantasy of helplessness or being abandoned or attacked. The search for power will not end as long as the fantasy lives. And while it lives the person is only half awake; his or her attention is split, as in a trance, between the inner fantasy and the outer world. The trance is subtle, unrecognized until it is broken, denied until it is seen.

These examples may or may not be convincing. They cannot substitute for the experience of realizing that one has been immersed in an unconscious fantasy while proceeding with one's life in the most normal way, thinking the same kinds of thoughts as everyone else. This "normal" trance does not preclude success, for the energy mobilized by fantasy may power action that results in abundant profit, fame, or conquest. Nevertheless, being absorbed in the trance is different from being "awake." The latter state, occasionally experienced by everyone, is perhaps a presage of the consciousness that is the aim of mysticism. Certainly, mystical consciousness is to be distinguished from accounts of "spiritual" experiences that are just more fantasies, more emotion-laden dreams of merging and dependency. The "blissed-out" disciple with a fixed smile revolves in a dream as deep as that of any demagogue caught up in power.

On those infrequent occasions when thought and fantasy subside, the observing self comes into prominence. One experiences the world with the vividness and rich detail that comes with fully attentive perception. However, this clarity does not last long. Bright as the world is, sooner or later one finds oneself reimmersed in fantasy, without any awareness of the transition, raising the question, "If the fantasy-free state is clear, rich, and bright, why would anyone resubmerge themselves in trance?" I suggest it is an automatic process to restore the object self, which recedes and disappears as perception becomes more "awake." Since fantasies support and strengthen the object self they are mobilized when its intensity falls below a certain level. That is why the more awake state tends not to last and the trance that had lightened deepens once again. Only as a different self comes into prominence will the power of the trance weaken and the awake state persist.

WAKING FROM THE TRANCE

In psychotic states, as in hypnosis, the dream of fantasy, the trance, is usually obvious, as is its interference with perception. With regard to normal consciousness, however, detecting the operation of the trance is more difficult, since "normal" is certified by consensus, and consensus is blind to its own limitations. But to the awakened person of mystical consciousness, the trance of ordinary life is quite apparent.

By referring back to the phenomenon of hypnosis we too can begin to see how ordinary consciousness may be an unrecognized condition of restricted awareness (Shor's and White's first criterion for a trance) in which what has faded away is *a much larger reality orientation,* a frame of reference that extends beyond the dimensions with which we are familiar. We can view the network of fantasies that influence our actions as hypnotic suggestions to which we comply. Thus, depending on the force of the fantasy that is active, we are likely to conduct most of our lives in a state of trance of varying depth, broken by interludes of relatively awake consciousness.

So habitual is the trance of ordinary life that one could say that human beings are a race that sleeps and awakens, but does not awaken fully. Because half-awake is sufficient for the tasks we customarily do, few of us are aware of the dysfunction of our condition. Moments of more complete awakening do occur, but the consensus of the group and the automatic functioning of the object self make such phenomena transient curiosities rather than urgent signals that something is wrong with the normal state.

Dreams can give us a taste of what our situation may be like. Shor, in comparing dreams and trance, described an incident of awakening from a dream and experiencing both waking reality and the dream reality simultaneously:

> In that fleeting instant I could compare the two worlds, and a startling comparison it was: two universes, fundamentally disparate, with different logic, different boundaries. Chiefly startling was the recognition that my dream was but an unkempt, faded world when compared against the vivid, detailed, unbounded waking world. Imagery was meager, background was hardly painted in.
>
> Nevertheless, during the dream itself the dream world had been an emotionally compelling world to dwell in. It was as vivid and as detailed as it needed to be in order to be totally "real" to me. Only when compared against waking standards did it seem restricted.[9]

The contrast is similar to that which mystics describe as existing between ordinary consciousness and the mystical. They suggest that just as a child is unaware of the more comprehensive awareness of an adult, the adult is unaware of the more extensive awareness of the person who has developed to another level. When we wake, we know we have been dreaming; while in the dream, there seems to be nothing else.

Although we value our brief moments of awakening for their clarity, vividness, and wider perception, we must realize that the goal of mysticism goes beyond what is possible to normal consciousness and beyond any simple idea of "being in the Now." A further development is intended. To bring that about, the object self must change from master to servant. The motivations derived from fantasy — jealousy, greed, pride, envy, hate — must be lessened so that persons may be capable of attending to more subtle stimuli than those to which their consciousness is attuned and restricted. In addition, the observing self must extend its range to free itself from the biases and assumptions of the culture. Only then will we have the capacity to awaken fully from the trance of ordinary life.

ANOTHER DIMENSION

The hidden world has its clouds and rain, but of a different kind.

Its sky and sunshine are of a different kind.

This is made apparent only to the refined ones — those not deceived by the seeming completeness of the ordinary world.

Rumi[10]

Part III
APPLICATIONS

10

Meditation

Meditation is the best known technique of mystical science, partly because of the emphasis it receives in the mystical literature and its capacity to produce impressive alterations in consciousness. It has come to be regarded as the essence of mystical science and persons who meditate may think of themselves as "spiritual" by virtue of that practice alone. Actually, meditation is just one component in a comprehensive program of development but one that is more easily specified than most of the other factors at work.

Since the early 1960s meditation has enjoyed wide popularity in the United States and is currently promoted through a variety of organizations. As a result it has become a subject for laboratory study and Western scientists have been able to establish that meditation produces "real" effects: physiological changes associated with relaxation and psychological effects of increased calm and enhancement of certain types of performance. Meditation is now regarded as a possible psychotherapeutic tool for wide application. When it is suggested that the mystical tradition might have a contribution to make to Western culture in general, and to psychotherapy in particular, most people think first of meditation techniques.

To assess the possible usefulness of meditation it is necessary to understand how it operates, which is not as difficult as might be imagined. Despite its exotic image, meditation is accessible to Western understanding, and I would like to offer a way of appreciating both its role in mystical science and its relationship to psychotherapy.

THE FUNCTION OF THE TWO TYPES OF MEDITATION

Although the variety of meditation procedures seems infinite, most writers on the subject divide them into two principal categories: concentration and mindfulness (or insight). Concentrative meditation focuses attention on a single target, such as a candle flame, a series of syllables spoken aloud or silently (a *mantrum*), an emotion such as reverence or love, or sensations such as those accompanying breathing or walking. Most Yogic meditations are concentrative. Mindfulness or insight meditation makes no attempt to control mind content but endeavors to maintain an even, uninvolved attentiveness to whatever thoughts, sensations, or emotions appear spontaneously. Most Buddhist meditations are of this type. Some forms of meditation seem to combine the two approaches, as when a sensory focus on breathing is coupled with noting the distractions that arise. But in no form of meditation does anyone engage in discursive, analytic thought. (Saint Ignatius called certain of his thinking exercises "meditations," but that usage is unusual.) Meditation is designed to counter the usual use of the mind for problem solving and conceptualization, activities especially marked in the West. However, Yogic and Buddhist meditations were originally designed for Easterners so it is clear that meditation addresses universal tendencies.

In my earlier research on meditation, I studied the responses of subjects who focused their attention on a blue vase.[1] The subjects reported changes in their perception that could be understood as a consequence of *deautomatization*, an undoing of the automatic processes that control perception and cognition.* For example, as they meditated the vase became more vivid, acquired lifelike properties, and called forth a mixture of sensory modalities ("I felt the light streaming from it"). By stopping thought and reinvesting percepts with attention, the meditators were reversing the normal developmental path by which one shifts attention from percepts to thought so that thinking activity can be enhanced. I postulated that deautomatization freed the person to perceive new aspects of their environment and thus could result in an expansion of perception.

Further studies pointed to a second, equally important activity of meditation: a shift from the object mode toward the receptive.[4] In most meditations, striving or grasping is given up and an attitude of allowing prevails. Problem solving and other future-oriented activities are set aside so that the meditator's mind is fully occupied with immediate reality. Instead of acting on the world (internal or external), the world is allowed to enter in and fill consciousness. As we have seen, the shift to the receptive mode carries with it a corresponding change in the perception of time, self, and meaning.

It is apparent to me that these two activities are secondary to a more important objective of meditation: the centering of the meditator in awareness rather than in mind content. Using the terms I have employed in this book, the principal aim of meditation is to enhance the observing self until its reality is without question and the meditator totally identifies with it. This permits the emergence of an entirely new form of consciousness called enlightenment, Nirvana,

---

*Deautomatization is a concept stemming from Hartmann's discussion of the automatization of motor behavior.[2] The concept was developed further by Gill and Brenman.[3]

awakening, and so forth. Thus, the two principal forms of meditation, concentration and mindfulness, can be understood as employing different means to achieve the same goal.

CONCENTRATIVE MEDITATION

Meditation's function of developing the observing self may not be obvious in meditation practices such as Transcendental Meditation (focusing on a mantrum) or its variations. Yet, if we turn to the texts of classical concentrative meditation we find a series of stages or levels of meditation in which the focus on a mantrum is the lowest, while the focus on pure awareness is the highest, stage.

The Visuddhimagga gives a detailed, explicit description of concentrative meditation as practiced by Buddhist monks in the fifth century. Differences exist between the Visuddhimagga and a text like the Yogic aphorisms of Pantanjali, but the basics are similar, proceeding from the more gross and superficial structures of consciousness to the more refined and basic.* Goleman's survey of meditation, based on the Visuddhimagga, is clear and succinct and provides a useful summary of the voluminous and dense original text. His summary traces the progression of stages:

> In the early stages of meditation there is a tension between concentration on the object of meditation and distracting thoughts . . . With much practice, a moment comes when these hindrances are wholly subdued. At this moment . . . one-pointedness and bliss . . . come into dominance.[5]

With continued practice the one-pointedness is sustained until

> The mind suddenly seems to sink into the object and remains fixed in it. Hindering thoughts cease totally. There is neither sensory perception nor the usual awareness of one's body: bodily pain cannot be felt . . . consciousness is dominated by rapture, bliss, and one-pointedness.[6]

---

*Concentrative meditation may also be employed for the development of special states of consciousness, as in Yogic meditation on the chakras, but eventually such states must be relinquished if "awakening" is to be attained.

The meditator proceeds to traverse and leave behind progressively more subtle and fundamental dimensions of experience. Rapture is superseded by bliss, which then gives way to equanimity, which, in turn, is left behind as one-pointedness is directed next to space, then to infinite awareness, then to the nonexistence of infinite consciousness. Each lower stage is seen as gross compared to the next higher one. At the end of the concentration path is a state described as neither perception nor nonperception; only the barest residuals of mental processes remain.

This last, the eighth stage, is not Nirvana, not the ultimate goal. According to the Visuddhimagga, that goal is attained by the practice of insight meditation, or mindfulness. The practice of concentrative meditation provides an excellent base for proceeding to insight meditation, but it is not completely necessary. A student can begin with mindfulness meditation although it will be slower going than for someone whose capacity for one-pointedness has already been developed. A person who has achieved the highest levels of concentration can quickly proceed to the highest levels of insight meditation and thus achieve the ultimate transforming experience.

From this Buddhist viewpoint, the crucial weakness of concentrative meditation is that the desire for personal gratification is suppressed rather than eliminated. However, it should be noted that in the Vedantic tradition, concentrative meditation is said to be capable of reaching the ultimate stage. The yoga of Pantanjali contains instructions for a progression of concentrative meditation practices leading to the cessation of the last vestige of desire and attachment and the development of *nirvakalpa samadhi*—becoming one with Brahman. Shankara describes the condition of the meditator who reaches this level:

Even though his mind is dissolved in Brahman, he is fully awake, free from the ignorance of waking life. He is fully conscious, but free from any craving. Such a man is said to be free even in this life.[7]

However, Pantanjali explicitly warned that without complete detachment: powers might be attained but not ultimate freedom,

When such concentration is not accompanied by non-attachment, and ignorance therefore remains, the aspirant will reach the state of the discarnate gods or become merged in the forces of Nature.[8]

INSIGHT MEDITATION

Insight meditation may have been developed because the powers and states that concentrative meditation produced proved to be too seductive and confusing.

Insight meditation attempts to strike at the root of desire. It seeks to bring about a total disinterest in self-gratification through the experience of all phenomena as transient and, therefore, unsatisfying.

To practice insight meditation, one should restrict one's attention to the bare notice of sensations and thoughts. One's attitude should be completely receptive to whatever contents arise in the mind. In the initial stages, the meditator notes and labels each content, for example, "anger" or "disturbing noise," and then dismisses it without judgment, repudiation, or pursuance. Mindfulness may be focused on body sensations as well, for example, noting each movement of the feet when walking slowly: "lifting," "swing," "down." Here too distracting thoughts or feelings may be noted, registered, and left behind. As this process goes on, the meditator has a succession of realizations about the nature of mind and self:

The first realization in insight is that the phenomena contemplated are distinct from the mind contemplating them . . . he can, with further insight, gain a clear understanding that these dual processes are devoid of self . . . Each moment of awareness goes according to its own nature, regardless of one's "will." It becomes certain to the meditator that nowhere in the mind can any abiding entity be detected . . . he knows "I am" to be a misconception.[9]

Here, it seems to me, the author of the Visuddhimagga perpetuates an error that is hard to avoid because our language is based on an object self, not on awareness, the observing self. Once again, the voice in the night declares that there is no voice in the night. "He knows 'I am' to be a misconception." Who knows that? How can awareness be said to arise and disappear like the objects of awareness: When awareness ceases, who is there to know it? By what means?

I suspect that lumping together the observing self with what is observed may be a matter of strategy rather than the result of empirical investigation. In the Buddhist view, as in mysticism in general, what we are accustomed to call real is seen as relatively unreal when compared to what is known through intuitive insight. Although the observing self is not an object and, thus, is not "of this world," it is not the state of enlightenment either, and teachers do not want their students to confuse one with the other so that they stop short of the goal. Therefore, the observing self is denied reality (permanency) along with what is observed. The beginning meditator may well think that awareness and its objects come into being and disappear together because he or she has little experience with awareness distinct from mental content. As insight meditation proceeds, however, that distinction becomes increasingly evident and awareness — the observing self — far from being transitory, becomes increasingly vivid and sustained.

Insight is now on the verge of its culmination; the meditator's noticing of each moment of awareness is keen, strong, and lucid . . . knows each moment to be impermanent, painful, or without self as *he sees* its dissolution [emphasis mine]. He sees all mental phenomena as limited and circumscribed, devoid of desirability, or alien. His detachment from them is at a peak. His noticing no longer enters into or settles down on any phenomena at all.[10]

This is the state from which the Nirvana experience is said to arise. Clearly, the observing self "knows" and "sees" mental phenomena arising and subsiding. When the observing self is complete, undiminished by "attachment," not "settling down" on any content, the meditator may gain access to a higher level of experience that transcends both mind content and the observing self.

To summarize, I am suggesting that the main activity of meditation is to develop the observing self. Concentrative meditation does this by focusing attention on a single content of consciousness — usually sensory — and then proceeding to discard, layer by layer, the mental strata that underlie it, until what remains is the light of awareness only. Mindfulness or insight meditation takes a different approach by establishing the distinction between the observer and the observed from the very beginning. Through the realization of the transiency of all mind content, it brings about a subsidence of desire for sensory and emotional phenomena and, finally, an almost total disappearance of mind content. This makes possible the next step, the arising of intuitive consciousness, called Nirvana or enlightenment or Truth.

It is the last step that really matters. From the point of view of mystical science, the other benefits of meditation, such as increased calm, improved physical health, or enrichment of associative thinking, are relatively trivial and can become hindrances if they are taken as the goals of meditation practice. Furthermore, practicing meditation for secondary purposes may later lessen its effectiveness for its primary purpose. One should keep these problems in mind when considering the use of meditation for psychotherapeutic, physical, or health purposes. Using a fine wood chisel to open tin cans makes sense only if you do not intend to do any carving and have no other means of opening cans.

THE USE OF MEDITATION
IN PSYCHOTHERAPY

Western psychotherapists who employ meditation in their practice regard it as an adjunct to psychotherapy, not a replacement for it. On the other hand, some teachers of traditions such as Tibetan Buddhism see meditation as a psychotherapy in its own right, and their discipline prescribes certain forms of meditation, practiced in designed environments, as treatment for specific conditions. These therapies have not yet been evaluated by Western psychological science. Even if such meditation procedures are effective therapies, few Western psychotherapists have the requisite training and experience to apply them with the skill needed. For these reasons, I will focus on the use of meditation as an adjunct to psychotherapy since that aspect of meditation is most likely to be significant for the reader.

Surveys of research on the therapeutic effects of meditation agree that repeating a mantrum or focusing on breathing sensations can produce changes of increased relaxation and calm in those who continue to practice them, resulting in improvement in conditions such as hypertension, anxiety, addiction, and phobias.[11, 12] Of course, these benefits accrue only to those who continue the practice, and many persons do not. Nevertheless, the results seem to confirm that meditation can be used as a treatment modality in suitable patients. Carrington and Shapiro both point out, however, that more recent studies comparing the effectiveness of meditation with other self-regulating strategies, such as EMG (electromyographic) feedback or progressive relaxation or even in one study, listening to music, show no difference between them in their effectiveness. Meditation is not a unique strategy for relaxation nor is it necessarily to be preferred to other approaches.[13] This finding should not be surprising since the originators of meditation techniques emphasized that physiological benefits were neither particularly significant nor the reason for practicing meditation.

As the mystical literature makes quite clear, the significance of meditation lies in its effect on the way a person experiences reality, the way his or her perception and understanding change. From this point of view, the work of Deatherage demonstrates the relevance of meditation for the practice of psychotherapy. Deatherage employed variations of mindfulness meditation as part of an ongoing, insight-oriented psychotherapy. In one type (Satipatthana), the meditator pays attention to breathing sensations and notes any thoughts or emotions that distract and interrupt continuous attention. The meditator attaches a label to these interruptions, for example, "worry," and then returns attention to the breathing. Two of Deatherage's case reports make clear the importance of the observing self, although in all the cases he cites, the meditator acquired more "distance" from symptoms.

In the first case, the patient suffered from anxiety, depression, loss of interest in life, and loss of self-esteem. She was hospitalized for severe depression and thoughts of self-destruction. In addition to the depression she complained of loss of concentration and racing thoughts:

> Mindfulness technique was presented to the patient as a "concentration exercise." She was asked to sit quietly, look at the second hand of an electric clock, and try to attend fully to its movement. She was instructed to notice carefully when she lost her concentration on the moving second hand, to identify what constituted the interruption, and to name it. She quickly found her concentration constantly broken by thoughts. On inspection, the nature of the thoughts

racing through her mind was always the same—concern with her past, her misfortunes in the relationship with her ex-husband, and her regrets about that situation.

She was instructed simply to label such thoughts, "remembering, remembering." The labeling process seemed to allow her to withdraw some of her involvement in those depressing thoughts about the past and to let her realize that more than just those thoughts was present in her mind; there was also a "she" who could watch and name thoughts. She learned to identify herself as the objective watcher of her disturbing thoughts instead of the depressed thinker, and she began to feel some relief from her psychiatric complaints . . .

With the additional benefits coming from the slightly disguised Satipatthana techniques, she could then investigate the nature of the watcher self which she had come to identify. This allowed her to come in contact with the calm and peaceful aspects of her own mind — her "center" was how she identified it at the time — and to re-establish some enjoyment and pleasure in her life.[14]

True to Buddhist doctrine, Deatherage is careful to point out:

When we employ mindfulness meditation with clinical patients, it is not our purpose to establish the watcher as anything permanent or "real."[15]

To the contrary, I would say that while the balance between awareness and the content of awareness may shift according to the needs of the situation, it is of utmost significance that the patient identify with the observing self rather than with the thoughts, emotions, and images that ordinarily occupy attention and reinforce the object self. The advantages of this discrimination are illustrated by Deatherage in the case of a woman who sought help for recurrent bouts of anxiety, especially in crowded places. Densensitization and simple counseling had failed to help.

After some preliminary sessions, we decided to try mindfulness techniques. She was shown the basic breath observation techniques of noting interruptions and naming them. After this, most sessions consisted of discussing her experiences with the mindfulness practices. After she had become fairly

adept at noting and naming interruptions to breath observation, and after the watcher had been investigated, she
began to work on observing emotions. She reported that,
as she sat quietly observing interruptions and emotions,
fear would arise within her from no detectable source,
panic would follow, and she would then have to struggle
with that anxiety — effectively ending her observation as
she became involved with the anxiety. Slowly she became
aware that the watcher could see but did not experience
anxiety, and she could sometimes get a little space between the "me" who was so afraid and the watcher.[16]

Following this insight, she progressed in her therapy.

If we consider the ways in which standard psychodynamic psychotherapy contributes to the development of
the observing self, we can see that Deatherage's use of meditation is but an extension of this process, a means of establishing
the posture of watching, that by shifting the center to that
which observes, the patient gains an increase of freedom from
the obsessive thoughts, emotions, and other content that had
previously dominated consciousness. This application of meditation seems to be more beneficial than using it primarily for
increased calm and relaxation, although these latter effects
can become a by-product of the observing position. Yet, it
seems to me that meditation used to enhance the observing
self is not really different from the central activity of Western
psychotherapy. The more such meditation is presented in
secular, modern form (such as watching the second hand of a
clock), the more it may be possible to integrate it into the
continuum of techniques that Western psychotherapists already employ to extract the observing self from the content
of awareness. In this way the exotic can become the familiar;
meditation — in its essentials — can join with the core of
Western psychotherapy.

REQUIREMENTS

The issues of adaptation and integration are all the more
important when we consider that meditation, as any pro-

cedure of mystical science, must be designed for the culture
and the individual to be most effective and not misused. Unfortunately, the adoption of classical techniques with all their
archaic trimmings is common practice in Western cultures
that are turning to the Eastern traditions. Common sense
suggests that meditation designed for a particular community
at a particular time in history is likely to have different effects
when applied to a different people in a different cultural
epoch. The need for specific adaptation is underlined by the
research of Daniel and Nina Freedman on differences in tem-
perament and behavior between Chinese and Caucasian babies:

> . . . they behaved like two different breeds. Caucasian
> babies cried more easily, and once started, they were
> harder to console. Chinese babies adapted to almost any
> position in which they were placed . . . rather than turning
> immediately to one side, as did the Caucasians.

When the babies' noses were pressed briefly, with a cloth, the
Caucasian babies fought, but:

> The average Chinese baby in our study simply lay on his
> back and breathed through his mouth, "accepting" the cloth
> without a fight. This finding is most impressive on film.

One test involved shining a light in the babies' eyes:

> It should be no surprise that the Caucasian babies continued
> to blink long after the Chinese babies had adapted and
> stopped.

Studies of Navaho newborns showed that they conformed to
the stereotype of the American Indian — stoical and impas-
sive — outdoing the Chinese babies in calm and adaptability.
The relative calmness of the Navaho babies compared to the
Caucasians extended even to the basic reflex response to
being dropped.[17]

   With these examples in mind it seems likely that any
one form of meditation (for example, sitting immobile and
counting breaths) will have different effects, depending on
the ethnic characteristics of the meditator. What is good for

one purpose for the Chinese or the Navaho may not achieve the same result for the Caucasion.

Western investigators agree that more research is needed to determine the specific effects of meditation and how it should be applied. Yet it is hard to find a single research paper that addresses the significance of the context within which the meditation procedure employed was originally developed and practiced or the instructions in the classical literature that specify the need for humility, selflessness, and sincerity. Ironically, although the power of meditation to affect physiological and psychological functions has been substantiated in many different laboratories, we have paid little attention to what the creators of meditation have said about its intended purpose and the requirements for its appropriate use. Their stress on motivational considerations has been ignored. Accordingly, the results of almost all meditation research have been compromised by insufficient focus on the attitude and purpose of the meditator.

Most people bring to meditation an acquisitive, self-centered orientation that is the cultural norm. According to the mystical literature, such an attitude determines the outcome of meditation. For this reason, the instructions that accompany the classical descriptions of meditation deal first with the necessity for "purifying the heart" — developing a selfless orientation — before aspiring to special powers. "Purifying the heart" is difficult for most people, usually requiring years of the right kind of effort. It is fair to say that such effort is not common among Western practitioners of meditation. The instructions also emphasize that meditation functions as only one component of an integrated, individualized system of development requiring the supervision of a teacher, someone whose perceptual capacity has been developed and who thereby can prescribe meditation according to the specific needs of the student.

Of course, if meditation is used for its lower-level functions and not pursued intensively, ignoring these instructions and cautions may not have much consequence. However, if one attempts to exploit potentially powerful meditation technology to its full extent, the needs both for the correct attitude on the part of the meditator (and the researcher) and for the guidance of a suitable teacher become increasingly important.

In this connection, a dramatic Tibetan story tells of a student who each day, while meditating in his room perceived a spider descending in front of him, growing larger and larger. He resolved to kill the spider and told his teacher of his plan to stab it the next time it lowered itself in front of him. The teacher instructed him to do nothing except draw a chalk mark on the spider's belly and then report back to him. When the student returned, the teacher told him to look at his own belly. The chalk mark was there.

From the point of view of Western psychology, the story shows the operation of projection: the student defended himself against hostile impulses of which he was unaware by hallucinating a spider. The source of the "danger" is shown to be inside the student. From the point of view of mystical science, the emotions and desires of the object self tend to distort and cloud perception. The story illustrates how this can lead to hurtful actions against what we perceive to be other people and beings but are in reality our self. The teacher can see what the student cannot and can therefore protect him or her from the consequences of confusion.

ADVERSE EFFECTS

In considering the potential usefulness of meditation for psychotherapy, we must recognize that some people are unable or unwilling to meditate. Most who start quit, in spite of obtaining initial benefits. Not everyone is improved by the experience; on the contrary, adverse effects are common. Some people find intensive meditation a convenient way to withdraw from social interaction and defend against intimacy. Good results are not guaranteed: certain meditations can increase obsessiveness and schizoid tendencies. Impressive altered states of consciousness are not necessarily accompanied by an increase in maturity. In fact, the reverse is just as likely. Misinterpretation of altered consciousness may result in an increase in grandiosity, magical thinking, and paranoia. Anxiety, even terror, may be occasioned by the weakening of conceptual and perceptual boundaries.

Adverse effects are almost certain for those who reason that if thirty minutes of meditation is good, three hours is better, and three days even more so. Such dubious logic seems to flourish in the field of esoteric practice. These people would not ordinarily consider taking one hundred aspirin simply because two had relieved their headache. Although they begin meditation on a modest enough scale, they soon proceed to gorge themselves. The result can be psychotic decompensation.

Because of these possible effects, authors who advocate meditation for psychotherapeutic purposes usually specify that the techniques be employed selectively by a therapist trained in the procedure and able to deal with idiosyncratic reactions.

The problems attendant to using meditation in psychotherapy are not limited to the patient. When the use of meditation is at variance with or unintegrated with the therapist's natural style and clinical training, the effect on the therapy is likely to be detrimental. As with any other intervention, the prescription of meditation by the therapist may be in the service of countertransference or overlook an impasse that should be explored and resolved. Equally important, the need for meditation techniques may be reduced or eliminated by a more adroit use of the therapist's own techniques and clinical knowledge. Unless these different considerations are borne in mind, the patient could easily end up with neither good meditation nor good therapy.

IMPROVING OUR APPROACH

It is safe to conclude that the benefits Western science has extracted from meditation are, thus far, insignificant. Classical meditation cannot be applied out of context and still produce the effects for which it was designed, namely, to aid the development of intuitive consciousness. Like any other powerful tool, meditation can be misused and its potential advantages wasted. Using it only for psychotherapy is like collecting oyster shells and throwing away the pearls. Persons employing it in this way are apt to conclude that the relatively trivial effects they obtain are the measure of mystical science, and they will look no further.

If Western psychological science is to gain more from meditation than the insignificant results we have obtained thus far, we cannot afford to select what attracts us from the technology of mysticism and discard the rest. We must pay attention to the mystical authors' requirements for meditation. We should seek qualified teachers and study and experience mystical science in order to understand the role of meditation as one component of a special body of knowledge. If we heed this advice, we will begin to take motivational dimensions as seriously as the physiological ones that we study so intensively and address ourselves to the covert purposes of persons who practice meditation, of researchers who study it, and of therapists who prescribe it. We will recognize the practical importance of shifting from an acquisitive orientation to one centered in learning and service.

After all, meditation, like mystical science in general, is not magic but a matter of personal development. Meditation can aid that process, but it cannot substitute for it. The basic issue is well known in the field of computer science, where similar magical expectations focus on the computer. Those who work with these elaborate machines remind themselves and others, "Garbage in — garbage out." Why should meditation be any different?

11

Teaching Stories

Teaching stories are found in all traditions: Vedanta, Buddhist, Zen, Hasidic, Christian, and, especially, the Sufi, in which large bodies of instructional material have been preserved and are still used. Most of the stories in this chapter are from the Sufis. Compared to meditation, teaching stories have received little attention from Westerners and are generally regarded as, at best, instructive parables or expressions of folk wisdom. Actually, they are far more sophisticated instruments than most people imagine. According to the Sufis, teaching stories can contain up to seven levels of meaning, constructed so that the reader or listener perceives the level that corresponds to his or her stage of spiritual development.

On its surface, the story can be humorous, moralistic, or entertaining, or a combination of these. Such elements ensure the story's survival. However, its teaching function depends on other qualities, one of which is the ability to portray a specific pattern of thinking or behavior. The auditor or reader registers the pattern unconsciously and when a corresponding situation arises he or she can recognize it. As a result, the person gains choice over previously automatic and unconscious behavior. He or she can observe and master the particular pattern. Thus, the domain of the observing self is extended to include the particular behavior and the person gains flexibility, autonomy, and effectiveness as the object self loses dominance. The teaching stories help to enhance the observing self step by step, preparing the way for further development of perception.

As an example, consider the following humorous story about Nasrudin, a fictional character whose comic exploits form an important body of teaching materials:

THE REASON

The Mulla went to see a rich man.

"Give me some money."

"Why?"

"I want to buy . . . an elephant."

"If you have no money, you can't afford to keep an elephant."

"I came here," said Nasrudin, "to get money, not advice."[1]

We can laugh as Nasrudin exposes his rationalization and greed for what they are. If he had really wanted to own an elephant he would have been more interested in the advice. He wants money; the elephant is just an excuse.

Having smiled at Nasrudin, we are able to smile in recognition of ourselves, when we rationalize a greedy wish. This recognition enables us to step aside from the behavior. We benefit because the tyranny of the object self has been diminished.

This deceptively simple story, a joke, also illustrates the way in which a teaching story contains meaning at more than one level. Nasrudin is also instructing us in the requirements for studying mystical science. Mystical teachers, like any other, are often approached by people who say they want one thing but really want another. Imagine a woman teacher (it is easy to forget that women as well as men have been teachers of mystical science) sought out by a man who says he wants one thing but really wants another. Such a supplicant may justify his request on the grounds that the wisdom he seeks to obtain from the teacher is to enable him to serve others or to further the spiritual salvation of the world. The teacher may tell him that until he has acquired some wisdom (money) of his own he will not have the means to make good use of hers. The seeker may well think, if not reply, "I came here for wisdom, not advice!"

This particular level of meaning lies just beneath the joke. Additional layers of meaning may be found depending on the experience one brings to the story and the care with which one considers the possible perspectives. "Earning" meaning yields a variety of insights whose impact will be far greater than that obtained if the interpretation were handed to the student like a sum of money. In working with this story, and with teaching stories in general, students learn through experience the important distinction between "Give me some money!" and "Teach me how to become rich." The former leads to dependency, the latter to independence. The stories are the tools, the means — they are not the money. Indeed, my explanation of "The Reason" decreases its potential usefulness to the reader by removing, to some extent, the opportunity for personal discovery of its meanings.

Remember that any explanation divides the whole into parts. The story's intended impact requires that its pattern be intact; when we disassemble it, as we might a watch, we find that the pieces are all there but the activity has ceased. Perhaps the following tale from the Hasidic tradition will help make clear the special communication a teaching story can provide, one not translatable into a didactic statement.

THE TREASURE

Rabbi Bunam used to tell young men who came to him for the first time the story of Rabbi Eisik, son of Rabbi Yekel in Cracow. After many years of great poverty, which had never shaken his faith in God, he dreamed someone bade him look for a treasure in Prague, under the bridge which leads to the king's palace. When the dream recurred a third time, Rabbi Eisik prepared for the journey and set out for Prague. But the bridge was guarded day and night and he did not dare to start digging. Nevertheless he went to the bridge every morning and kept walking around it until evening.

Finally the captain of the guards, who had been watching him, asked in a kindly way whether he was looking for something or waiting for somebody. Rabbi Eisik told him of the dream which had brought him here from a faraway country. The captain laughed: "And so to please the dream, you, poor fellow, wore out your shoes to come here! As for having faith in dreams, if I had had it, I should have had to get going when a dream once told me to go to Cracow and dig for treasure under the stove in the room of a Jew — Eisik, son of Yekel, that was the name! Eisik, son of Yekel! I can just imagine what it would be like, how I should have to try every house over there, where one half of the Jews are named Eisik, and the other Yekel!" And he laughed again. Rabbi Eisik bowed, traveled home, dug up the treasure from under the stove, and built the House of Prayer which is called "Reb Eisik's Shul."

"Take this story to heart," Rabbi Bunam used to add, "and make what it says your own: There is something you cannot find anywhere in the world, not even at the zadik's and there is, nevertheless, a place where you can find it."[2]

No explanation, no direct statement of the story's meaning can substitute for the way it acts on the reader's mind. The story provides an *experience* of meaning. Here too, there is more than one level, depending on the symbolism and technical use of such words as *king's palace, bridge, dream,* and *under the stove.* Teaching stories are designed to have a series of specific impacts, directed at a developmental goal. Their special activity is what makes them technical instruments, provided they are constructed by someone who knows how they function, for what purpose they are needed and can put them into a form suitable to the time and culture in which they are to be employed.

BYPASSING THE LEFT HEMISPHERE

Contemporary research on the different modes of operation of the two hemispheres of the brain provides a basis for appreciating the potential of teaching stories. It has been demonstrated that each hemisphere of the brain processes information in a distinct, specialized way. For most people, the left hemisphere functions in a linear, analytic, sequential mode that corresponds roughly to the object mode of consciousness. Logic, mathematics, and verbal syntax are the specialties of the left hemisphere.

In contrast, the right hemisphere responds to spatial aspects of experience, to patterns or designs, to what is taken as a whole — the simultaneous, the symbolic. Its specialties are artistic functions and orientation in space. For example, recognizing faces and appreciating music are functions of the right brain.

In experiments where normal persons receive certain information in their right brain only, that information is shown to be perceived *outside* the subjects' immediate awareness — as an impression or sense of something that they cannot verbalize. For example, in research performed by Roger Sperry, a subject was presented with a series of images of neutral objects. Interspersed in the series was a picture of a nude woman. The images were presented first to the left brain and then to the right and the subject was asked what she saw. When the picture was flashed to the left brain the subject laughed, declaring, "It's a nude!" When the picture was flashed to the right brain, the subject said that she saw nothing, but almost immediately a sly smile spread over her face and she began to chuckle. Asked what she was laughing at, she said: "I don't know . . . nothing . . . Oh — that funny machine!"[3]

The problem for the left hemisphere, with its more analytic, linear mode, is to be able to register and articulate information from the right, even though the form of that information does not fit the left hemisphere's mode of organization. Julian Jaynes has suggested that at one time a much freer communication existed between the hemispheres in human beings, with the right brain being experienced as a hallucinated voice, ascribed to a god.[4] Whether or not he is correct, it is likely that the capacity to make effective use of right-brain functions (and we are far from knowing all that they entail) requires both sensitivity to right-brain cues and the discrimination of such cues from other subtle inputs. Teaching stories may help us to discriminate right-brain input by heightening our sensitivity to the contaminating influence of emotions and motivations on our perception. To be open to right-brain input without becoming the pawn of emotions and desires requires that we suspend or limit left-brain dominance at the same time we avoid being misled by the unrecognized effect of emotions and desires on perception. After all, a principal function of the left hemisphere is to maintain a realistic course of action rather than engage in purely emotional, impulsive activity. Teaching stories can help to attain the necessary detachment and discrimination because they heighten sensitivity to the contaminating influence of covert motivations.

ALL YOU NEED

"I'll have you hanged," said a cruel and ignorant king, who had heard of Nasrudin's powers, "if you don't prove that you are a mystic."

"I see strange things," said Nasrudin at once; "A golden bird in the sky, and demons under the earth."

"How can you see through solid objects? How can you see far into the sky?"

"Fear is all you need."[5]

It is also possible that the multilevel structure of teaching stories enables the left hemisphere to make better use of the right-hemisphere mode. In ordinary information processing, the difference in functions of the two halves of the brain can produce competitive interference. Levy and his colleagues commented on this problem:

The two hemispheres may process the same sensory information in distinctly different ways...the two modes of operation, involving spatial synthesis for the right and temporal
analysis for the left, show indications of mutual antagonism.
The propensity of the language hemisphere to note analyt-
ical detail in a way that facilitates their description in
language seems to interfere with the perception of the
overall Gestalt, leaving the left hemisphere "unable to
see the woods for the trees."[6]

A teaching story, by presenting left- and right-hemisphere information simultaneously, occupies the dominant left side
with the processing of its own type of material, thus reducing
left-side interference with the spatial-holistic information that
can be utilized by the right side.

For example, in "The Treasure," the events are told in
a linear (left-hemisphere) mode. It progresses in time and
ends; the dialogue is logical, featuring reasoning and planning.
The interrelation of its elements, however, is of a different
order. It is a pattern whose vivid impact depends on holding
in awareness, simultaneously, the paradoxical elements that
turn the flow of events into a circle rather than a straight line.
The story communicates something that is hard to think
about in a logical sequence, hard to "grasp." The Gestalt, the
overall configuration, is processed by the right hemisphere.*

Ornstein and his co-worders obtained empirical data
supporting this hypothesis by comparing the EEG alpha responses of subjects given Sufi stories to read with their responses to reading a technical report. They found significantly
more right-hemisphere involvement in reading the stories
than in reading the technical material.[7]

Further evidence supports the hypothesis that teaching
stories make use of left/right cognitive differences. Otto
Poetzel's experiments, later replicated and extended by

*A familiar example of this nonlinear structuring is the Arabian Nights format of
a tale within a tale within a tale, the conclusion of each being delayed and linked
with the next, in tangential fashion.

Fisher, demonstrated that visual information processing depends on whether the information is perceived at the center of the visual field or at the periphery. When subjects viewed a picture and were asked to describe it from memory, the details they did *not* describe appeared in their dreams that night.[8] Later experiments showed that the phenomenon occurred because the unreported details occupied a peripheral position in the subjects' attention fields. The missing information appeared in the nonlinear, more holistic style of dream thought.

The following story illustrates this issue; its latter half contains a commentary on itself and on teaching stories in general.

THE DESIGN

A Sufi of the Order of Nagshbandis was asked: "Your Order's name means, literally, 'The Designer.' What do you design, and what use is it?"

He said: "We do a great deal of designing, and it is most useful. Here is a parable of one such form.

"Unjustly imprisoned, a tinsmith was allowed to receive a rug woven by his wife. He prostrated himself upon the rug day after day to say his prayers, and after some time he said to his jailers:

" 'I am poor and without hope, and you are wretchedly paid. But I am a tinsmith. Bring my tin and my tools and I shall make small artifacts which you can sell in the market, and we will both benefit.'

"The guards agreed to this, and presently the tinsmith and they were both making a profit, from which they bought food and comfort for themselves.

"Then, one day, when the guards went to the cell, the door was open and he was gone.

"Many years later, when this man's innocence had been established, the man who had imprisoned him asked him how he escaped, what magic he had used. He said:

" 'It is a matter of design, and design within a design. My wife is a weaver. She found the man who had made the locks of the cell door, and got the design from him. This she wove into the carpet, at the spot where my head touched in prayer five times a day. I am a metal-worker, and this design looked

to me like the inside of a lock. I designed the plan of the arte-
facts to obtain materials to make the key—and I escaped.' "

"That," said the Nagshbandi Sufi, "is one of the ways in
which a man may make his escape from the tyranny of his
captivity."[9]

Just as the astute tinsmith was able to see the possibilities in
details the guards did not notice, so the right hemisphere may
be able to use information that the left hemisphere cannot.
Right-hemisphere information can be encoded in details that
form the design needed to escape.

Careful attention to the details of this story reveals a
multitude of themes woven into its rich and complex fabric,
including the psychological captivity of human beings, the
need to trick our captors, the function of prayer, the role of
intuition, the importance of involvement "in the world," the
necessity of paying attention to subtle aspects of experience,
and the "hidden" nature of mystical knowledge. The charac-
ters in teaching stories are often designed to represent different functions of the mind. The events of such a story may also
portray the evolution of the individual or the human race.

To harvest what stories like "The Design" can yield, it
is necessary to appreciate the skill and artistry with which it
is constructed, its carefully chosen phrases and sequences,
and the possibility of a radical, unfamiliar perspective contained in its depths. Time, repeated readings, balancing the
usual analytic attitude with the receptive, and calm, un-
hurried interest are essential.

TEACHING STORIES IN PSYCHOTHERAPY

Teaching stories in appropriate modern translations
may prove to be more compatible with psychotherapy than
meditation, since they are consonant with our insight-oriented
culture and not overly magical. Here again, as in meditation,
we are not yet equipped to employ them directly as therapeutic tools. Their principal value lies in their ability to

heighten therapists' awareness of their self-deceit. As an example, consider my use of the following story:

VANITY

A Sufi sage once asked his disciples to tell him what their vanities had been before they began to study with him.

The first said, "I imagined that I was the most handsome man in the world."

The second said, "I believed that, since I was religious, I was of the elect."

The third said, "I believed that I could teach."

The fourth said, "My vanity was greater than all these; for I believed that I could learn."

The sage remarked, "And the fourth disciple's vanity remains the greatest, for his vanity is to show that he once had the greatest vanity."

After reading this story, I observed myself doing the same thing as the fourth disciple by berating myself excessively for a personal failing. As I was doing so, the story came to my mind like a mirror, and I understood the role of vanity in what I was doing. The context was different from the specific situation of the story, but the dynamics were similar. My understanding provoked a wry smile and ended my self-flagellation. Not long afterward, a male patient presented feelings of self-blame whose concealed vanity I was able to recognize, for the pattern was the same. He was castigating himself for having made a "mess" of his opportunities, particularly as he was generally recognized as being highly intelligent and likable. After listening to him for a while, I offered an alternative view: "I think you're doing yourself an injustice. You're not a good guy who is making a mess of things — you're a mess who is doing a good job!"

He stopped in his tracks, wide-eyed, then threw back his head and roared with laughter. In the next session, he reported that he felt much better and had reduced his self-recriminations noticeably. My recognition of his concealed vanity, followed by an appropriate interpretation, was matched by his own recognition and decrease in his symptom. A behaviorist might say I had applied an aversive stimulus and therefore extinguished the response — a case of instrumental conditioning. I think not. Judging by my own experience, the "stimulus" does not feel aversive at all; it feels like relief, for it is recognition. The source of the distress suddenly becomes clear and the distress itself disappears, leaving a delightful sense of new freedom. The relief is more than temporary, for the observing self gains new ground.

I did not have the patient read the story. That would not have been as effective, nor was it necessary. All I had to do was perceive what was taking place, then intervene therapeutically. Teaching stories can best assist the psychotherapist in this way. By broadening and deepening the therapist's own perception, they make it possible to address additional dimensions of the patient's situation.

CONCLUSION

As I have indicated, teaching stories may be likened to templates to which we match our own behavior. We accept them because they are deceptively impersonal; they are presented as the histories of other people. The story slides past our vigilant defenses and we store it in our minds until the moment when our own thinking or situation matches the template. Then it suddenly arises in awareness and we "see," as in a mirror, the shape and meaning of what we are actually doing. Enhancement and further development of the observing self — with concomitant reduction in the controlling power of the object self — probably constitute the most important immediate benefit to be obtained by using these materials. Teaching stories may be more practical for most people than meditation because they address behavior in everyday life where wisdom must be applied and tested. Teaching stories also supply special input in the form of right hemispheric cognition. According to the Sufis, such stories can affect the latent intuitive function of our minds, providing a type of "nutrition" needed for its development. Teaching stories are tools whose effectiveness depends on the motivation of the user and his or her capacity for understanding. As that understanding increases, the user can apply the tools to finer and deeper work.

Thus, the teaching story is a far more sophisticated technical device than most people appreciate. However, one must be aware that not all stories qualify in this respect. Some are adulterated or watered down; some are expressed in a vernacular or style that is no longer effective. As with other components of mystical science, teaching stories must be adapted to the current needs and situations. These materials, when suitably selected and translated for modern audiences, offer us a valuable resource. Fully consonant with our literate culture, they are, in my opinion, the best available introduction to mystical science.

Teaching stories have one other significant function different from those considered above: the "Moses' basket effect." If the story is entertaining enough, if it captures the interest and memory of the reader or hearer, it will be preserved and passed on — with its hidden information and power — to succeeding generations. When formal religious and scientific texts may be confiscated and destroyed, it will be immune from censorship because its surface is so innocuous and challenges no doctrine. Thus, the teaching story preserves priceless information. With this in mind, perhaps we can sense the encoded riches contained in this concluding story:

THE PRECIOUS JEWEL

All wisdom, according to Daudzadah, is contained in the various levels of interpretation of this ancient traditional tale.

In a remote realm of perfection, there was a just monarch
who had a wife and a wonderful son and daughter. They
all lived together in happiness.

One day the father called his children before him and
said:

"The time has come, as it does for all. You are to go
down, an infinite distance, to another land. You shall seek
and find and bring back a precious Jewel."

The travelers were conducted in disguise to a strange
land, whose inhabitants almost all lived a dark existence.
Such was the effect of this place that the two lost touch
with each other, wandering as if asleep.

From time to time they saw phantoms, similitudes of
their country and of the Jewel, but such was their condition that these things only increased the depth of their
reveries, which they now began to take as reality.

When news of his children's plight reached the king, he
sent word by a trusted servant, a wise man:

"Remember your mission, awaken from your dream, and
remain together."

With this message they roused themselves, and with the
help of their rescuing guide they dared the monstrous
perils which surrounded the Jewel, and by its magic aid
returned to their realm of light, there to remain in increased happiness for evermore.[11]

12

Mysticism and Psychotherapy

CONSCIOUS EVOLUTION

The perspective of mysticism is evolutionary, although not Darwinian in the sense of relying on natural selection alone and having no prefigured ends. A further distinction is that Darwin opposed the idea of evolutionary "progress," of designating "higher" and "lower" species, with human beings at the top. Mysticism, on the other hand, does acknowledge a higher state of intuitive knowing versus a lower one restricted to intellect and sensory perception. On such a scale of consciousness, animals are lower than humans, and plants and minerals are lower still. Mystics believe that all levels constitute stages in a continuous line of upward progress whose further development is not biological but psychological. That further development depends on a dynamic that is not selective adaptation based on reproductive success, as in Darwin's theory, but *conscious evolution*: human beings evolving themselves through a special type of learning that they choose to acquire.

So considered, our further evolution is a bootstrap operation. The human organism, having first learned to regard itself as an object in order to survive in the biological world, must take the next step of learning that it is *more* than an object. To do so requires that it use its intellect to demonstrate the limitations of intellect and to encourage itself to seek something transcending the patterns of thought with which it is familiar. The task is not easy. Thought alone cannot really convince us that our object self is just a temporary convenience, since thought and language are based on the behavior of physical objects. Likewise, perception and imagery are shaped by objects and present us with a time-bound world with discrete boundaries. To perceive ourselves as more than objects and to sustain that perception for more than brief moments requires a radically different form of perception, a form of knowing that is not subservient to ordinary mental processes. Mystics assert that this is possible, but is there any evidence supporting the idea that human beings can develop in themselves a new form of perception, one that is latent but requires special conditions for its development?

It has long been claimed that human beings have unused mental capacities. Such claims are usually based on the huge number of neurons in the central nervous system and the enormous number of their possible combinations. Recently, however, science has accumulated a body of neurophysiological research that supports the thesis that we have unused, undeveloped capacities that could be "awakened" under the right conditions.[1] For example, researchers have found that more nerve-to-muscle connections exist in newborn than in adult rats. Gradually, as rats mature, the multiple pathways drop out until there is a one-to-one pattern: one nerve to one muscle. This finding suggests that more connections exist initially than are eventually needed; as the animal matures the excess is "pruned." Presumably, a process of selective preservation is at work, an hypothesis confirmed by studies of the optic pathways of monkeys. It was found that the visual system of monkeys is somewhat disorganized at birth: connections from the brain to the right and left eyes are mixed together; in the adult they are separated. It appears that the same process of selective preservation operates in the monkey's perceptual system as in the rat's muscle system.

It could be argued, however, that the loss of neurons was programmed genetically and not related to the experiences of the developing animals. To investigate this possibility, further experiments were performed in which one eye of newborn monkeys was closed for a prolonged period, changing the pattern of selective loss. The result was that the connections from both sides to the open eye *increased*, while the connections to the closed eye almost all disappeared and it became blind. Greenough and Juraska comment:

> These findings suggest that the developing animal comes equipped with a broad range of potential brain-organization patterns, not all of which are necessary in any one environment. Patterns activated by the animal's experience become strengthened and refined, while those that remain unused are lost or weakened.[2]

Several hundred years ago, the mystic Rumi stated:

> New organs of perception come into being as a result of necessity.
> Therefore, O man, increase your necessity, so that you may increase your perception.[3]

Clearly, Rumi could not very well evoke "synapses," "dendritic spines," or "pyramidal neurons." But if we compare his statement to the conclusion reached by Greenough and Juraska, we may begin to wonder: Are we possessed at birth of neuronal circuits with a developmental potential for the kind of direct, intuitive knowing that mystics say is possible? Is the development of this potential dependent, in part, on stimuli and requirements imposed by the environment? Can that potential be revived by specific exercises that would make special demands on the organism? Would the development of that capacity have its own requirements involving diminished activity of competing circuits?

If the answer to these questions is yes, the esoteric doctrines and practices of the mystical tradition cease to seem as esoteric or irrational. They can be viewed as skillful means for a perceptual development discovered in ancient times and transmitted through the symbols, artifacts, and metaphors indigenous to the particular culture in which the science was practiced. As strange and unscientific as mystical procedures may appear, especially when viewed apart from the system in which they were integrated, we may find their effects reflected in neurophysiological changes associated with an increased range of function of the brain.

MYSTICISM AND ITS CONTEXT

With this research in mind we can begin to understand and accept the statement made much earlier that mystical science is not dependent on the use of a religious or "spiritual" vocabulary or context. It can be, and has been, expressed in other formats. It is a special psychology whose operation derives from the new perception it brings about. For example, if a teacher perceived that a student needed to develop the capacity for diligence — and if it were the Middle Ages — the teacher might assign him or her the task of hand copying and illuminating a religious document. In the twentieth century, however, a real teacher would not prescribe an activity suitable to a thousand years earlier but would make an assignment appropriate to the culture and the person — perhaps giving the student the task of rebuilding an automobile engine in a repair shop or doing research on a topic in learning theory in a university library. There is no intrinsic need for religious dogma, asceticism, mysterious costumes, or other customary features of a theological context. In the past, mystics often scandalized the religious community of which they were considered a part by their practices of writing and reciting erotic poetry, wearing ordinary dress, exhibiting "insane" behavior, and showing complete unconcern for the religious affiliations and beliefs of their students. Although the profound perception of reality achieved by mystics formed the basis for most formal religions, the association with religion that is now so firmly fixed in people's minds is unnecessary and, usually, a hindrance. Mystical science projected in nonreligious formats has existed throughout history and undoubtedly exists now, unrecognized.

At the same time, it is easy for contemporary persons to assume that mysticism can be adequately explained in terms of their own scientific framework, whether that be psychological, neurobiological, or both. Indeed, such persons may feel that their analysis is superior to what the mystics have to say about their own discoveries. The authors of the mystical texts have been well aware of this problem and warn that their science is not reducible to any set of formal principles or formulas that purport to explain what it does and how. Thus, propositions such as those I have culled from the mystical literature and the translations I have made of them into the framework of Western psychology will be most helpful if they are employed as a bridging framework rather than as a conclusive analysis. In truth, the essence of mysticism cannot be indicated directly:

STRIKE ON THIS SPOT

Dhun-Nun the Egyptian explained graphically in a parable how he extracted knowledge concealed in Pharaonic inscriptions.

There was a statue with pointing finger, upon which was inscribed: "Strike on this spot for treasure." Its origin was unknown, but generations of people had hammered the place marked by the sign. Because it was made of the hardest stone, little impression was made on it, and the meaning remained cryptic.

Dhun-Nun, wrapped in contemplation of the statue, one day exactly at midday observed that the shadow of the pointing finger, unnoticed for centuries, followed a line in the paving beneath the statue.

Marking the place he obtained the necessary instruments and prised up by chisel blows the flagstone, which proved to be the trapdoor in the roof of a subterranean cave which contained strange articles of a workmanship which enabled him to deduce the science of their manufacture, long since lost, and hence to acquire the treasures and those of a more formal kind which accompanied them.[4]

ENGAGING IN THE BOOTSTRAP

As a theory, the evolutionary perspective of mysticism need not be more convincing than any other intellectual schema. It acquires reality only as one actively engages in the bootstrap operation. To illustrate how this might take place, suppose one were to study and work with teaching stories such as those I have quoted. Gradually, over time, one would gain a heightened awareness of how beliefs and perceptions can distort or deny reality in the service of acquisitive motives or of fear or vanity — all servants of the object self. That awareness would lead to an increasing appreciation of the corruptness and bias in much of our thought and opinions. As a consequence, the authority of those thoughts — our conceptual prison — would be reduced and new possibilities seen.

As I indicated earlier, we are familiar with a parallel process in psychotherapy in which unconscious fantasies, emotions, and strategies are brought into awareness with a consequent gain in freedom and a diminution of symptoms. However, we have not had the means to extend that process to the cognition of everyday life or to our hidden cultural and scientific prejudices. Mystics compare the problem to that of a stone held so close to the eye that nothing else can be seen. When the stone is held further away, the world comes into view.

Acquiring distance from our preoccupations and automatic patterns of thought is what I have called the strengthening and extending of the observing self. Mystical science, by increasing the scope of observation to include the conceptual prison, can assist the therapist and the lay person alike to realize how they are confined and how to escape. We gradually come to understand that meaninglessness and the despair of "I am alone" are products of obscured vision and inappropriate extrapolation of rules governing objects, rules that are useful only for a narrow range of phenomena. As one continues to participate in the bootstrap process, the idea of conscious evolution makes increasingly good sense because that is what seems to be happening to one, at least in a modest way.

To the extent that therapists understand this wider context, their work will be oriented by a basically positive and optimistic perspective, instead of covertly supporting meaninglessness and existential despair.

Thus, the value of mysticism for psychotherapy lies not in the application of its technical devices to patients, as if those devices were a mental antibiotic or a superior tranquilizer, but in the change that mystical science can bring about in the therapist's world view and concept of the possibilities of human life.

CAN MYSTICISM REPLACE PSYCHOTHERAPY?

Although the evolutionary perspective indicates that enlightenment or Nirvana is not an end state, for in the framework of linear time the process is infinite, the mystical literature does describe the awakening of intuitive perception as a point of radical transition. It is said to bring an end to the suffering typical of the human condition in its undeveloped state. For example, Buddha advised, "Therefore . . . everyone should seek self-realization . . . the Truth that ends all pain . . . Transcendent Truth that spans the troubled ocean of life and death . . ."[5]

Typically, the enlightened yogi or Zen monk is depicted as serene, joyous, and freed from ordinary cares. Given such a beneficial effect of mystical development on human suffering, the question of whether mysticism can replace psychotherapy arises naturally. However, the more pertinent question is, "Who wants psychotherapy and who wants mysticism?" The fact is that the goal of mystical practice is reached by the annihilation of self-centeredness — something most people are not interested in, at least initially. Furthermore, although "awakening" is presented in a positive way and is said to free a person from suffering, it requires a different orientation than that of seeking personal benefit, namely, the wish to learn who one is and where one is going. In contrast, persons seeking psychotherapy suffer from painful symptoms that interfere with work, intimacy, and pleasure. Such people are necessarily intensely focused on themselves; they seek immediate relief from their suffering as well as the satisfaction of frustrated longings. They do not have the energy and interest to spare for the relatively disinterested learning needed to benefit from mysticism's teachings.

One must deal with first things first. Even if people are not suffering acutely but, rather, turn to mysticism to experience strange states of consciousness or to socialize or to obtain approval, they will probably be disappointed, unless they join one of the many organizations that cater to such wishes and are not mystical at all except in their outer trappings.

Mystical science is for those who can obtain satisfaction of their worldly needs from appropriate sources and do not seek them, in disguise, in the spiritual domain. Worldly needs must be satisfied elsewhere so that their pursuit does not interfere with the learning process. Similarly, psychopathology must be dealt with first. Consequently, there is no way for mysticism to substitute for psychotherapy, or vice versa.

THE CONTRIBUTION OF PSYCHOTHERAPY

The question of whether psychotherapy can contribute to mystical science is also relevant. The answer to this question begins with the recognition that greed, heedlessness and arrogance — attitudes that prevent a student from absorbing mystical teaching — have their roots in anxiety, fantasy, and the neurotic distortions of reality with which psychotherapy deals. Greed, for example, frequently results from a persistent dependency orientation, a feeling that someone else must supply what is needed; that unhappiness can be banished by swallowing something; or that security is a matter of accumulation. Psychotherapy can reduce the intensity of such processes, reduce neurotic self-centeredness, correct misinterpretations of the world that began in childhood, and teach new strategies that are more effective in meeting a person's needs. When this work is accomplished, a person will be more apt to approach mystical science for what it is intended to offer and be able to function as a student. Genuine students need not be entirely free of egocentricity, but just free enough to keep it from overwhelming the more subtle communication that mystical schools employ. Psychotherapy can help people attain the degree of objectivity necessary for effective participation in mystical studies.

THE OBSERVING SELF AS BRIDGE

The observing self provides a place from which the arbitrary, the transient, and the limited can be assessed. By means of the observing self, ongoing life experiences can be used to gain understanding of the human condition. As one begins to realize the effect of motivation on the way we experience ourselves and the world, one can progress away from the preoccupations of the object self (being self-centered) to serving the task (being selfless). The farther one progresses, the better the alignment of one's activity with the fundamental, dynamic field in which we exist. Through that experience one can know a larger reality and a larger self.

The thought self, the emotion self, the action self, and the observing self are complementary phases of consciousness; they are not the fundamental source of individual being. That source is beyond ordinary awareness; mystics call it the Self or Truth or Knowledge. The ability to perceive the Self is the product of mystical development. Undoubtedly, this fundamental reality transcends the four selves and the boundaries of the individual human being as well. The experience of the Self provides knowledge of the unity of life, leading to such pronouncements as "God is One" or "I am the Truth." The observing self can be a bridge between the object world and the transcendent realm. Without the enhancement and development of the observing self, the further step to the Self cannot be taken.

We cannot say exactly what the observing self *is*, but our inability to do so tells us something. It indicates that the accepted psychological model of human beings is deficient in a basic way. It points to an unknown region whose exploration requires a radically different model of the self, one in which "simple locality" is no longer assumed and the world view of mystics becomes a useful guide.

THE INDIVIDUAL TASK

Mystical science is a complex, integrated, organic whole. It involves far more than the stereotyped drama in which a solitary individual locates a mystical master and after long trials is rewarded with enlightenment. According to such fables, mystical development is an isolated transaction between disciple and guru. Yet the mystical literature describes the practice of mysticism quite differently. It uses the metaphor of making bread to illustrate the progressive stages of work that must be accomplished in the process. First fields must be plowed, then the seed sown, and in due time the grain harvested. Next the grain is ground into flour, and the flour mixed with salt and yeast and placed in the oven to bake. Only then does one obtain a loaf of bread that will provide the nourishment to sustain and advance life. These stages apply to entire civilizations as well as to individuals.

It can be misleading to think that anyone can know the Self, for that knowledge is not simply a product of one individual's effort or ability. The necessary base must be present in the culture, the time must be right, and a suitable group of qualified persons must function together to perform in the correct way the work of development. At present our society is probably at the stage in which the field needs to be plowed or the grain sown. In this context, the role of individual students of mysticism may be to assist in that process, even if the bread is not baked until later generations.

This perspective differs sharply from the popular notion that enlightenment is out there in the possession of some sage who decides to bestow it on the best disciple. Yet the more complex and long-range view of mystical development expressed in the metaphor of making bread is both realistic and hopeful. It allows people to be what they can be and to do what they, and only they, can do.

In the Bhagavad Gita we find, "Better is one's own dharma, though imperfectly performed, than the dharma of another well performed."[6]

From the Sufi tradition, "To be a Sufi is to become what you can become and not to try to pursue what is, at the wrong stage, illusion."[7]

In a Hasidic anecdote, "Before his death, Rabbi Zusya said, 'In the coming world, they will not ask me: Why were you not Moses? They will ask me: Why were you not Zusya?' "[8]

Mystical science is a developmental process, not a particular dogma or technique. It does not exist in isolation from the larger community in which it operates. Its perspective spans many generations and so should our own, especially when we consider the meaning of our individual lives. If we proceed in the direction indicated by the mystical tradition, we will have enough work to do to occupy our energies for a long time to come. There is no need to pursue the exotic, the alien. There is a need to make better use of what our sciences have taught us and to assimilate the knowledge and perspective of the mystical tradition into Western psychology and Western society. The harvest of our efforts will be a deeper understanding of human life and the capacity to further its evolution.

Appendix—Selecting a Mystical School

Some readers may wish to investigate mystical science and wonder whether they should enroll in one of the numerous spiritual groups, cults, or religious organizations that have proliferated recently. With regard to most such groups, the answer is no. As I hope I have already made clear, the appearance and label of a group or person is no guarantee of viability, of the capacity to bring about the development with which mysticism is concerned. In fact, the more such a group conforms to the popular fantasy of the mystical, the less likely it is to be effective.

Would-be students of mystical science must make their own assessment, as best they can, of a mystical group's genuineness in order to conserve their time and resources. The accuracy of that assessment will depend on their ability to discriminate between their legitimate wish to learn and their co-existing wishes for attention, entertainment, power, and so on. "Greed makes you believe things you would not normally believe."[1] Our reason is often the servant of our wishes and nowhere more so than in the general area of the mystical. If we cannot tell when our lower aspirations are operating, we may easily misinterpret our attraction to a particular group and its teacher as being an "intuitive" recognition of its genuine mystical nature. For this reason, the more self-knowledge a person has the better his or her chance of success. Like Nasrudin seeking money to buy an elephant, one must have some money of one's own to start with.

When making inquiries of a group purporting to teach mystical knowledge, it can be useful to ask such questions as the following:

1. Does the group operate in such a way as to help new members clarify their motivations for joining the group or does it assume that they are just showing good judgment? If the latter is the case, be wary.

2. Does the group provide members with the means for seeing and understanding the motivational patterns of ordinary living? If not, be wary.

3. Does the group gratify wishes for dependency, new experiences, emotional excitement, special status, and vanity? If so, steer clear of it.

4. Does the group employ emotional arousal, repetition, guilt, and the use of group approval or disapproval? These are the principal components of thought reform (brainwashing) or conversion processes.

Careful attention to these points will help a would-be student of mystical science to avoid the numerous ineffective organizations that serve to fulfill the more primitive needs of both student and teacher but do not serve the aim of conscious evolution. Still, it is important to recognize that cults and religious organizations of various kinds do perform important functions for their members. They satisfy members' needs for acceptance and protection and often provide members with a disciplined, healthy routine of balanced living, good diet, and exercise. By also providing security, firm direction, and a controlled community life they can have a psychotherapeutic effect, reducing anxiety and teaching more adaptive behavior. The group's dogma can provide a framework of meaning and hope absent in the lives of many of its members prior to joining. At the least, such groups provide distraction, entertainment, and social opportunities.

The worst offer group and parental security at the price of destructive regression.

But whatever the actual nature of a particular group, if a student covertly desires what it offers, he or she will find the group satisfactory. The traditional dictum, "If you are sincere you will find your teacher" or "The Teacher will find you" can be understood to mean that what you actually are seeking is the only thing you will find. You and your teacher will deserve each other — whatever the purpose that unites you.

One reason for widespread self-deceit in the area of spiritual development is that people have been trained to feel ashamed of "lower" wishes, despite the fact that such wishes have their own place and function. We need a certain amount of social gratification, emotional stimulation, attention, self-esteem, and security. But a notion of the "spiritual" has arisen in which all these needs are supposed to be cast behind one, like the devil. As a consequence, people pretend to have the "right" (that is, "higher") motives. As a result, they seek one thing in the guise of another and neither objective is obtained as efficiently and successfully as it might be.

Classically, mystical schools dealt with the problem of self-deceit in a variety of ways. One approach was to provide what the inappropriately motivated students wanted and thus to keep them occupied while the real spiritual teaching took place out of sight with qualified students. Another technique was for the school to present an unattractive, that is "worldly," appearance so that the unqualified would go elsewhere. Still another method was to refuse to provide what the student wanted until he or she gave up and went elsewhere. In other words, genuine mystical schools arrange things so that the students sort themselves out.

Although cults and religious groups meet certain of the needs of people seeking whatever it is they happen to offer, they create a serious problem for those with the potential for studying the real science. For such people, entanglement with "dead" organizations can be damaging. To begin with, all groups exert pressure on their members to conform to group values. This pressure serves the group's primary motive (usually unconscious) of self-perpetuation. In addition, members rigorously adhere to group norms, since the latter reassure them of their identity. A particularly clear example of the operation of such norms is the stereotyped dress and language of "revolutionary" groups; in such organizations, rebellion against the outside world may be encouraged, but it is never tolerated against the group itself.

The pressure on the members of the group to conform is difficult to withstand. This factor may not matter too much for ordinary purposes, but for the effective operation of mystical science such pressure is detrimental, since it serves the relatively crude motives of dependency, desire for approval, and so on. Not only are these motives reinforced, but discovery of them is made more difficult, for it is not in the group's interest for the members to become aware of what is actually taking place. Even worse, groups often make the gratification of such egocentric desires acceptable by labeling the process "spiritual." As a result, members may believe that the limited effects of the group, of outdated techniques, uninformed meditation practices, dances, and the like, represent the true measure of mystical science. Under such circumstances, a student will unknowingly remain trapped in a sterile situation, losing the chance to develop further, or will drop out altogether, concluding that mysticism is a fraud or a form of psychopathology.

Thus, the serious student must not only scrutinize carefully the operation of a spiritual group, but must be especially observant in assessing his or her own reactions. "Am I excited at the prospect of strange states of consciousness? Am I happy to have found a smiling teacher who welcomes me and gathers me into the fold? On the other hand, am I attracted by a group that makes it hard to enter, treats me harshly, requires sacrifices?"

By rigorously observing both the group in question and oneself, the very process of surveying the spiritual marketplace can be more valuable than the benefits a given group may actually offer. Thus, the process of assessment can provide the initial lessons in learning how to learn from one's own experience, the skill that viable mystical schools are most concerned to teach.

Notes

MOTTO

Haidar Ansari, trans. and ed., in "Voice in the Night," *Wisdom of the Idiots,* 2d ed. (London: Octagon Press, 1971).

CHAPTER 1 – AN INVITATION

1. H. Ellenberger, "Psychiatry from Ancient to Modern Times," in *The American Handbook of Psychiatry*, vol. 1, ed. S. Arieti, (New York: Basic Books, 1974), p. 6.

2. E. Durkheim, *The Elementary Forms of the Religious Life* (New York: Free Press, 1965).

3. W. Hunt and A. Issacheroff, "History and Analysis of a Leaderless Group of Professional Therapists," *American Journal of Psychiatry* 132(11) (1975); 1166.

4. T. Lidz, "On the Life Cycle," in *The American Handbook of Psychiatry*, vol. 1, ed. S. Arieti, p. 251.

5. E. Schrodinger, *What Is Life? Mind and Matter* (London: Cambridge University Press, 1969), p. 149.

6. M. Greene, ed., *Toward a Unity of Knowledge*, Psychological Issues 6(2) (New York: International Universities Press, 1969), p. 48.

CHAPTER 2 – MYSTICISM AS A SCIENCE

1. M. Polanyi, *Personal Knowledge* (Chicago: University of Chicago Press, 1958).

2. H. Dingle, *The Scientific Adventure* (New York: Pitman, London Philosophical Library, 1953), pp. 38-39. Cited in D. Rapaport, *The Structure of Psychoanalytic Theory*, Monograph 6, 2:2, (New York: International Universities Press, 1960), p. 142.

3. P. Kapleau, *The Three Pillars of Zen* (Boston: Beacon Press, 1967), p. 173.

4. W. Heisenberg, *Physics and Philosophy* (New York: Harper and Brothers, 1958), p. 106.

5. Dogen, in R. Masunaga, *The Soto Approach to Zen* (Tokyo: Layman Buddhist Society Press, 1970), p. 88.

6. S. Nikhilananda, *The Upanishads*, vol. 1 (New York: Bonanza Books, 1949), p. 205.

7. I. Shah, *The Magic Monastery* (New York: E. P. Dutton, 1972), p. 13.

CHAPTER 3 – PSYCHOTHERAPY AS AN ART

1. H. Ellenberger, "Psychiatry from Ancient to Modern Times," in *The American Handbook of Psychiatry*, vol. 1, ed. S. Arieti (New York: Basic Books, 1974), pp. 3–20.

2. Editor's introduction to "Project for a Scientific Psychology," in *The Standard Edition of the Complete Psychological Works of Sigmund Freud*, vol. 1, ed. J. Strachey (London: Hogarth Press, 1964), p. 293.

3. M. Lampert, A. Bergin, and J. Collins, "Therapist-induced Deterioration in Psychotherapy," in *Effective Psychotherapy*, ed. A. Gurman and A. Razin (New York: Pergamon Press, 1977), pp. 452–481.

4. K. Mitchell, J. Bozarth, and C. Drauft, "A Repraisal of the Therapeutic Effectiveness of *Associate* Empathy, Nonpossessive Warmth, and Genuineness," in *Effective Psychotherapy*, ed. A. Gurman and A. Razin, pp. 482–502.

5. Ibid., p. 498.

6. M. Polanyi, *Personal Knowledge* (Chicago: University of Chicago Press, 1958).

7. H. Ellenberger, *The Discovery of the Unconscious* (New York: Basic Books, 1970), pp. 47–48.

8. W. Condon, "Multiple Responses to Sound in Dysfunctional Children," *Journal of Autism and Childhood Schizophrenia*, 5:1 (1975), 37–56.

CHAPTER 4 – THE ORIGINS OF MYSTICISM

1. S. Rao, "Indian Philosophy," *The Encyclopaedia Britannica*, vol. 12 (Chicago: Encyclopaedia Britannica, 1951), p. 248.

2. S. Prabhavananda and C. Manchester, trans., *The Upanishads: Breath of the Eternal* (New York: New American Library, 1957).

3. W. Rahula, *What the Buddha Taught* (New York: Grove Press, 1959), pp. 36–37.

4. I. Richards, *The Republic of Plato* (New York: W. W. Norton, 1942), pp. 131–133.

5. I. Shah, *The Way of the Sufi* (New York: E. P. Dutton, 1970), p. 80.

6. Ibid., p. 110.

7. Ibid., p. 102.

CHAPTER 5 – INTUITION

1. S. Freud, "New Introductory Lectures on Psycho-Analysis," in *Standard Edition of the Complete Psychological Works of Sigmund Freud*, vol. 22, ed. J. Strachey (London: Hogarth Press, 1964), p. 66.

2. I. Shah, *Tales of the Dervishes* (London: Jonathan Cape, 1967), p. 207.

3. W. Morris, ed., *American Heritage Dictionary of the English Language* (Boston: Houghton Mifflin, 1969), p. 1086.

4. Ibid., p. 688.

5. M. Westcott, *Toward a Contemporary Psychology of Intuition* (New York: Holt, Rinehart and Winston, 1968), p. 6.

6. B. Jowett, Trans., *The Dialogues of Plato, Great Books of the Western World*, vol. 7, ed. R. Hutchins (Chicago: Encyclopaedia Britannica, 1952), p. 180.

7. I. Richards, *The Republic of Plato* (New York: W. W. Norton, 1942), p. 192.

8. F. Waters, *The Book of the Hopi* (New York: Ballentine Books, 1963).

9. A. Wolf, "The Life and Writings of Spinoza," in *The Encyclopaedia Britannica*, vol. 21 (Chicago: Encyclopaedia Britannica, 1951), pp. 235–236.

10. B. Russell, *A History of Western Philosophy* (New York: Simon and Schuster, 1945), p. 708.

11. R. von Mises, "Mathematical Postualtes and Human Understanding," in *The World of Mathematics*, vol. 3, ed. J. R. Newman (New York: Simon & Schuster, 1956), p. 1743.

12. W. Barrett and H. Aiken, *Philosophy in the Twentieth Century: An Anthology*, vol. 3 (New York: Random House, 1962), pp. 303, 305.

13. Freud, "New Introductory Lectures," p. 159.

14. H. Hartmann, *Essays on Ego Psychology* (New York: International Universities Press, 1952).

15. E. Kris, *Psychoanalytic Explorations in Art* (New York: International Universities Press, 1952).

16. J. Campbell, ed., *The Portable Jung* (New York: Viking Press, 1971), p. 114.

17. Ibid., p. 221.

18. J. Bruner, *On Knowing: Essays for the Left Hand* (Cambridge: Harvard University Press, 1963), p. 102.

19. Ibid., p. 20.

20. Westcott, *Toward a Contemporary Psychology*, p. 22.

21. F. Vaughan, *Awakening Intuition* (Garden City, N.Y.: Anchor Press/Doubleday, 1979).

22. L. Le Shan, *The Medium, The Mystic and the Physicist* (New York: Viking Press, 1974).

23. F. Capra, *The Tao of Physics* (Berkeley, Calif.: Shambala, 1975).

24. G. Zukav, *The Dancing Wu Li Masters: An Overview of the New Physics* (New York: William Morrow, 1979).

25. M. Greene, ed., *Toward a Unity of Knowledge*, Psychological Issues 6(2) (New York: International Universities Press, 1969), p. 45.

26. M. Polanyi, *Personal Knowledge* (Chicago: University of Chicago Press, 1958), p. 131.

27. Greene, *Toward a Unity of Knowledge*, p. 60.

28. A. Whitehead, *Science of the Modern World* (New York: Macmillan, 1960), pp. 71–72.

29. Le Shan, *The Medium, the Mystic and the Physicist*, p. 138.

30. Ibid., p. 275.

31. W. Heisenberg, *Physics and Philosophy: The Revolution in Modern Science* (New York: Harper and Brothers, 1958).

32. L. Bertalanffy, *Problems of Life* (New York: Wiley, 1952), p. 124.

33. Ibid., p. 134.

34. Capra, *The Tao of Physics*, p. 138.

35. B. d'Espignat, "The Quantum Theory and Reality," *Scientific American*, November 1979, pp. 158–181

36. *Science News*, August 22, 1981, p. 117.

37. B. d'Espignat, *Conceptual Foundation of Quantum Mechanics*, 2d ed. (Reading, Mass.: W. A. Benjamin, 1976), p. 291.

38. D. Thomsen, "Mystic Physics," *Science News,* August 4, 1979, p. 94.

39. J. Bernstein, "A Cosmic Flow," *American Scholar*, Winter 1978/79, pp. 6–9.

CHAPTER 6 – THE OBJECT SELF

1. M. Von Senden, *Space and Sight* (Glencoe, Ill.: Free Press, 1960).

2. P. Wolff, *The Causes, Controls and Organization of Behavior in the Neonate*, Psychological Issues 5:1. Monograph 17 (New York: International Universities Press, 1960).

3. R. Spitz, *The First Year of Life* (New York: International Universities Press, 1965), p. 41.

4. J. Piaget, *The Origins of Intelligence in Children* (New York: International Universities Press, 1952), pp. 331-338.

5. L. Ames, "The Sense of Self of Nursery School Children as Manifested by Their Verbal Behavior," *Journal of Genetic Psychology* 81 (1952): 193–232.

6. A. Gesell, *The First Year of Life: A Guide to the Study of the Pre-School Child* (New York: Harper and Row, 1940), p. 32.

7. Ibid., p. 37.

8. Ames, "The Sense of Self," p. 229.

9. Ibid., p. 232.

10. H. Norton, *Translations from the Poetry of Rainer Maria Rilke* (New York: W. W. Norton, 1962), p. 181.

11. D. Shapiro, "A Perceptual Understanding of Color Response," in *Rorschach Psychology*, ed. M. Richers-Ovisiankina (New York: Wiley, 1960), pp. 154–201.

CHAPTER 7 – MOTIVATION, VIRTUE, AND CONSCIOUSNESS

1. I. Shah, *The Way of the Sufi* (New York: E. P. Dutton, 1970), p. 164.

2. S. Nikhilananda, *The Upanishads*, vol. 1 (New York: Bonanza Books, 1949), pp. 187–188.

3. S. Suzuki, Lecture, July 1968, Zen Mountain Center, *Wind Bell* 7:28 (1968).

4. Nikhilananda, *The Upanishads*, vol. 2 (New York: Ramakrishna-Vivekananda Center, 1952), p. 33.

5. M. Buber, *Tales of the Hasidim — Later Masters* (New York: Schocken Books, 1948), p. 86.

6. M. Buber, *Tales of the Hasidim — Early Masters* (New York: Schocken Books, 1948), p. 312.

7. R. Spitz, *The First Year of Life* (New York: International Universities Press, 1965), p. 48.

8. Ibid., p. 50.

9. Shah, *The Way of the Sufi*, p. 165.

10. D. Goddard, ed., *A Buddhist Bible* (Boston: Beacon Press, 1970), p. 102.

11. L. Kohlberg, "Moral Development and Identification," National Society for the Study of Education, *Yearbook*, 1962, pp. 277–332.

12. Ibid.

13. L. Kohlberg and D. Elfenbein, "The Development of Moral Judgments Concerning Capital Punishment," *American Journal of Orthopsychiatry* 45(4) (July 1975): 514–540.

CHAPTER 8 — THE OBSERVING SELF

1. R. Maharshi, *Talks with Sri Ramana Maharshi* (Tiruvannamalai: T. N. Venkataraman, Sri Ramanasraman, 1972).

2. *The Standard Edition of the Complete Psychological Works of Sigmund Freud*, vol. 18, ed. J. Strachey (London: Hogarth Press, 1955), p. 238.

3. Ibid., vol. 16, 1963, p. 287.

4. Ibid., vol. 12, 1958, p. 135.

5. R. Ladouceur, "Habit Reversal Treatment: Learning an Incompatible Response or Increasing the Subject's Awareness," *Behaviour Research and Therapy* 17(4) (1979): 313–316.

6. F. Perls, *Gestalt Therapy Verbatim* (Lafayette, Calif.: Real People Press, 1969), p. 30.

7. Ibid., p. 43.

8. Ibid., p. 44.

9. Ibid., p. 49.

10. A. Miller, K. Issacs, and E. Haggard, "On the Nature of the Observing Function of the Ego," *British Journal of Medical Psychology* 38 (1965): 161-169.

11. H. Kohut, *The Analysis of the Self* (New York: International Universities Press, 1971), p. xv.

12. C. Evans, *The Subject of Consciousness* (New York: Humanities Press, 1970).

13. Ibid., p. 104.

14. Ibid., p. 149.

15. G. Globus, "On 'I': The Conceptual Foundations of Responsibility," *Archives of General Psychiatry*, 137(4) (April 1980): 417-422.

16. Miller et al., "The Observing Function of the Ego."

17. Ibid.

18. J. Blofeld, *The Zen Teaching of Huang Po* (New York: Grove Press, 1959), pp. 49, 56.

19. W. Yeats, *The Collected Poems of W. B. Yeats* (New York: Macmillan, 1951), pp. 327-328.

20. I. Shah, *The Way of the Sufi* (New York: E. P. Dutton, 1970), p. 219.

CHAPTER 9 – THE TRANCE OF ORDINARY LIFE

1. R. White, "A Preface to the Theory of Hypnotism," in *The Nature of Hypnosis*, ed. R. Shor and M. Orne (New York: Holt, Rinehart and Winston, 1965), p. 207.

2. R. Shor, "Hypnosis and the Concept of the Generalized Reality-Orientation," in *The Nature of Hypnosis*, ed. Shor and Orne, pp. 291, 295.

3. R. Shor, "Three Dimensions of Hypnotic Depth," in *The Nature of Hypnosis*, ed. Shor and Orne, p. 313.

4. M. Orne, "The Nature of Hypnosis: Artifact and Essence," in *The Nature of Hypnosis*, ed. Shor and Orne, pp. 89-123.

5. T. Sarbin, "Contributions to Role-taking Theory: I. Hypnotic Behavior," in *The Nature of Hypnosis*, ed. Shor and Orne, p. 249.

6. Shor, "Three Dimensions of Hypnotic Depth," p. 314.

7. M. Erickson, E. Rossi, and S. Rossi, *Hypnotic Realities* (New York: Wiley, 1976), p. xviii.

8. J. Haley, *Uncommon Therapy* (New York: W. W. Norton, 1973), pp. 21-22.

9. Shor, "Three Dimensions of Hypnotic Depth," p. 313.

10. I. Shah, *The Way of the Sufi* (New York: E. P. Dutton, 1970), p. 104.

CHAPTER 10 – MEDITATION

1. A. Deikman, "Experimental Meditation," *Journal of Nervous and Mental Disease* 136 (1963): 329-343.

2. H. Hartmann, *Ego Psychology and the Problem of Adaptation* (New York: International Universities Press, 1958), pp. 88-91.

3. M. Gill and M. Brenman, *Hypnosis and Relaxed States* (New York: International Universities Press, 1959), p. 178.

4. A. Deikman, "Bimodal Consciousness," *Archives of General Psychiatry* 25 (December 1971): 481-489.

5. D. Goleman, *The Varieties of the Meditative Experience* (New York: E. P. Dutton, 1977), p. 11.

6. Ibid., p. 13.

7. S. Prabhavananda and C. Isherwood, *How to Know God: The Yoga Aphorisms of Pantanjali* (New York: New American Library, 1953), p. 64.

8. Ibid., p. 32.

9. Goleman, *The Varieties of the Meditative Experience*, p. 24.

10. Ibid., pp. 30-31.

11. P. Carrington, *Freedom in Meditation* (Garden City, N.Y.: Anchor Press/Doubleday, 1977).

12. D. Shapiro and D. Giber, "Meditation and Psychotherapeutic Effects," *Archives of General Psychiatry* 36 (March 1978): 294-302.

13. M. Raskin, L. Mi Bali, and H. Peeke, "Muscle Biofeedback and Transcendental Meditation," *Archives of General Psychiatry* 37 (January 1980): 93-97.

14. S. Boorstein, *Transpersonal Psychotherapy* (Palo Alto: Science and Behavior Books, 1980), pp. 177-178.

15. Ibid., p. 178.

16. Ibid., p. 186.

17. D. Freedman and N. Freedman, "Ethnic Differences in Babies," *Human Nature* 2(1) (January 1979): 36–44.

CHAPTER 11 – TEACHING STORIES

1. I. Shah, *The Pleasantries of the Incredible Mulla Nasrudin* (London: Jonathan Cape, 1968), p. 13.

2. M. Buber, *Tales of the Hasidim – Later Masters* (New York: Schocken Books, 1948), p. 245.

3. M. Gazanaga, "The Split Brain in Man," in *The Nature of Human Consciousness*, ed. R. Ornstein (San Francisco: W. H. Freeman, 1973), p. 98.

4. J. Jaynes, *The Origin of Consciousness in the Breakdown of the Bicameral Mind* (Boston: Houghton Mifflin, 1976).

5. I. Shah, *The Exploits of the Incomparable Mulla Nasrudin* (New York: E. P. Dutton, 1972), p. 138.

6. Cited in D. Galin, "Hemispheric Specialization: Implications for Psychiatry," *Archives of General Psychiatry* 31 (October 1974): 573.

7. R. Ornstein, J. Herron, J. Johnstone, and C. Swencienis, "Differential Right Hemisphere Involvement in Two Reading Tasks," *Psychophysiology* 16(4): 398–401.

8. O. Poetzl et al., "Preconscious Stimulation in Dreams, Associations, and Images," *Psychological Issues* 2(1) (1960): 18.

9. I. Shah, *Thinkers of the East* (London: Jonathan Cape, 1971), p. 176.

10. I. Shah, *The Magic Monastery* (New York: E. P. Dutton, 1972), p. 47.

11. Shah, *Thinkers of the East*, p. 123.

CHAPTER 12 – MYSTICISM AND PSYCHOTHERAPY

1. W. Greenough, "Development and Memory: The Synaptic Connection," in *Brain and Learning*, ed. T. Teyler (Stamford, Conn.: Greylock Publishers, 1978), pp. 138–145.

2. W. Greenough and J. Juraska, "Synaptic Pruning," *Psychology Today*, July 1979, p. 120.

3. I Shah, *Tales of the Dervishes* (New York: E. P. Dutton, 1970), p. 197.

4. Ibid., p. 55.

5. D. Goddard, ed., *A Buddhist Bible* (Boston: Beacon Press, 1970), p. 86.

6. S. Nikhilananda, *The Bhagavad Gita* (New York: Rama-krishna-Vivekananda Center, 1952), p. 119.

7. R. Ornstein, *The Mind Field* (New York: Grossman/Viking, 1976), p. 105.

8. M. Buber, *Tales of the Hasidim — The Early Masters* (New York: Schocken Books, 1948), p. 251.

APPENDIX — SELECTING A MYSTICAL SCHOOL

1. I. Shah, *Wisdom of the Idiots* (New York: E. P. Dutton, 1970), p. 107.

Arthur J. Deikman, M.D., associate clinical professor at the University of California, San Francisco, has conducted groundbreaking scientific investigations into meditation, altered states of consciousness, and mysticism. The author of *Personal Freedom* and coauthor of *Symposium on Consciousness,* Deikman combines teaching and writing with the practice of psychiatry.